WORDSWORTHIAN
AND OTHER STUDIES

WORDSWORTHIAN

AND OTHER STUDIES

BY

ERNEST DE SELINCOURT

LATE PROFESSOR OF POETRY IN THE
UNIVERSITY OF OXFORD
AND PROFESSOR OF ENGLISH IN THE
UNIVERSITY OF BIRMINGHAM

OXFORD
AT THE CLARENDON PRESS
1947

OXFORD UNIVERSITY PRESS
AMEN HOUSE, E.C. 4
London Edinburgh Glasgow New York
Toronto Melbourne Cape Town Bombay
Calcutta Madras
GEOFFREY CUMBERLEGE
PUBLISHER TO THE UNIVERSITY

PRINTED IN GREAT BRITAIN

C

PREFACE

I HAVE assembled in this posthumous volume such of
Ernest de Selincourt's essays and lectures as I have
reason to think he would have approved for preservation.
The volume presents on a rather wider canvas than that
of the *Oxford Lectures*, published in 1934, the character
of his mind and the range of his interests. The delightful discourse on *The Art of Conversation* will recall to
those who knew him something of the quality of his own
talk with its light play of irony, its literary flavour, its
wit and wisdom.

I acknowledge with gratitude permission to publish
kindly granted by the Princeton University Press (for
Wordsworth and His Daughter's Marriage), the English
Association (for *The Early Wordsworth* and *Coleridge's
Dejection: An Ode*), the Oxford University Press (for
Landor's Prose and *Walt Whitman*), the Editor of 'The
Hibbert Journal' (for *The Interplay of Literature and
Science during the Last Three Centuries*), and the
Registrar of the University of Liverpool (for *The Art
of Conversation*).

HELEN DARBISHIRE

CONTENTS

I

THE EARLY WORDSWORTH[1]

WORDSWORTH has often been abused for the arrangement of his poems under the headings of *Poems of Childhood, of Fancy, of Imagination, of Sentiment and Reflection,* and so on, but his most captious critic would hardly question the appropriateness of the title given to his first section—*Poems written in Youth.* That section closes with *The Borderers,* which was completed at Racedown in the last months of 1796. These 'Juvenile Pieces', as he calls them, contain, indeed, some notable things, for had not Coleridge, some two years back, detected in the *Descriptive Sketches* the 'emergence of an original poetic genius', and when, on his visit to Racedown, *The Borderers* was read aloud to him, did he not pronounce it to be 'absolutely wonderful'? But it was not till the spring of 1797 that Wordsworth could free himself from the disturbing effects of those two profound shocks from which his moral and spiritual nature had suffered—the first, dating from February 1793, when war broke out between his beloved native country and France, the land of his ideals; the second, even more severe, some eighteen months later, when the French, betraying their creed of universal freedom and brotherhood, 'became aggressors in their turn', and 'changed a war of self-defence to one of conquest'. Forced to renounce his faith in the Revolution, Wordsworth fell back in his disillusionment upon a barren intellectualism which failed to satisfy his nature, and then,

> perplexed with contrarieties
> Yielded up moral questions in despair.

His recovery was slow, and the verse he wrote bore traces of his sickness, so that when, in *The Prelude,* he

[1] Presidential address to the English Association, 1936.

came to take stock of the past, he saw the years spent at
Racedown as years of spiritual convalescence, in which

> gleams of light
> Flash often from the east, then disappear,
> And mock me with a sky that ripens not
> Into a steady morning.

What was true of his spiritual sanity he felt in after-life
to have been true also of his theory and practice of
poetry and of poetic style. Critics have seen in his
latest work a departure from the ideals and practice of
his prime. Wordsworth saw none himself. 'No change',
he asserted in 1843, 'has taken place in my manner for
the last 45 years.' He himself recognized only one point
of cleavage in the continuity of his poetic life; he dated
it from his residence at Alfoxden in 1797. He was then
in his twenty-eighth year. How many of our contemporary poets would be content to dismiss all that they
had written up to the age of twenty-seven as *Juvenilia*?
Let us admit that Wordsworth was slow to develop:
perhaps he had a deeper and more varied experience,
both of books and life, to assimilate than some of his
successors; and until it was assimilated, he was not fully
himself.

But while he draws a line thus definitely between his
poetic apprenticeship and his maturity, no one has believed, nor taught us to believe, more firmly in the
significance of the formative years. 'The child is father
of the man', and the man is moulded by the natural and
intellectual environment of childhood. At first this is
unconsciously absorbed, and like the chameleon he takes
his colour from what he feeds on; then, as the critical
faculty awakens, he makes a conscious selection from
the many and varied influences about him, and even
violently reacts from some of them. And if the man
is a writer, whose instrument is language, the same
process is at work in the formation of his vocabulary and
style. For style is the reaction of his personality to the

various linguistic influences, both written and spoken, to which he has been subjected, and his language is a sure indication not only of the company he has kept, but also of that part of the company that he has preferred. Hence the early crudities of a great and original poet have a value irrespective of their intrinsic merit in the light they throw upon that fascinating and, as I think, illuminating study, the growth of a poet's mind and art.

Of that growth Wordsworth has himself left a priceless record. But though in *The Prelude* he treats exhaustively of what he owed to Nature, he gives less detail of his literary education. He acknowledges, indeed, a debt to books, even from the 'years of infancy and prattling childhood', and pays magnificent tribute to the poets, as Powers

> For ever to be hallowed, only less
> For what we may become and what we need,
> Than Nature's self, which is the breath of God;

but he tends to run away from the subject; so that, after writing over six hundred lines under the heading *Books*, he is forced to admit that

> Thus far a scanty record is deduced
> Of what I owed to books in early life,
> Their later influence [i.e. upon his youth and early
> manhood] yet remains untold.

I propose to do a little, this afternoon, towards filling in these gaps, and to tell you something of what can be learnt of the years of his apprenticeship from a perusal of certain unpublished manuscripts that have passed through my hands.

But first let me summarize what is already common knowledge. His infant reading was in the old-world nursery tales, Jack the Giant-killer, St. George, Robin Hood, and the like; at the age of eight he had a passion for the *Arabian Nights*; by the time he was thirteen he had already absorbed *Gulliver's Travels* and *The Tale of a Tub*, much of Fielding and other eighteenth-century novelists which he found in his father's library. At about the same age[1] he began to love poetry, and to find 'in words of tuneful order, sweet for their own sakes, a passion and a power'. Before this he had learnt by heart, at his father's instigation, extracts from Shakespeare, Spenser, and Milton; and it was doubtless some of these that he would recite to his school-friend as they walked round Esthwaite together in the early morning, reading and repeating their favourite verses. But much must have been the work of his less eminent contemporaries, for, as he admits, the objects of his boyish love were 'often false and in their splendour overwrought'; indeed, at this callow age, what else could be expected? At fourteen he began to write himself. A poem on the summer vacation was set as a school task, and to this, on his own initiative, he added verses on his Return to School. To the next year belongs his first extant poem. The school at Hawkshead had been founded by Archbishop Sandys in 1585, and when the boys were invited to celebrate its bicentenary, the young Wordsworth produced a copy of verses in the approved commemorative manner. In later years he spoke slightingly of them. 'They were', he said, 'much admired, far more than they deserved, for they were but tame imitation of Pope's versification, and a little in his style.' But this is too severe. Of course they are imitative, how better could a young poet learn his trade than by sitting at the feet of his great predecessors? And for a theme of this kind he chose the obvious best model. Thus speaks his Goddess of Education:

> Then noble Sandys, inspir'd with great design
> Rear'd Hawkshead's happy roof, and call'd it mine.

[1] So *The Prelude* (1805), V. 575. 'Thirteen years or haply less.' The text of 1850 reads 'Twice five years or less,' but in matters of detail the text of 1805 is generally more trustworthy.

There have I loved to show the tender age
The golden precepts of the classic page,
To lead the mind to those Elysian plains,
Where, throned in gold, immortal Science reigns;

—an admirable sentiment, on which the Goddess, with all her new-fangled theories, has not improved in these latter days. It is, moreover, expressed with spirit, with a good sense of metre, a command of language, and a feeling for the well-turned phrase. He has clearly read Pope and his followers to some profit. 'It was the success of this poem', he tells us, 'that put it into my head to compose other verses from the impulse of my own mind.' Some of these still survive, dating from his sixteenth and seventeenth years.

The best of them, both in form and style, follow classical models. Of his play-hours *The Prelude* preserves full and vivid recollections—any one of us, I suppose, if called upon to recount the incidents of boyhood, would find his memory following the same course. And so Wordsworth tells us much of his youthful escapades, of ranging the hills for woodcocks, of boating and riding in the summer, of skating in the winter, of games of loo and whist and even noughts and crosses on stormy evenings, of cakes and sweets, of 'plates of strawberries and mellow cream', but very little of his lessons. Of the school curriculum he merely remarks that he 'might easily have fed upon a fatter soil of Art and Letters', and he leaves it at that. This was ungrateful of him. He did not realize, as others have certainly not realized, how much he owed to a sound early training in the classics. If he was never a scholar in the technical sense, it is clear that even at school he acquired enough knowledge to make the literature of the past a reality to him, and that all through the years of his apprenticeship he kept up the practice of translation and imitation, thereby advancing in mastery of his own individual art. He speaks himself deprecatingly of the 'trade in classic niceties', with 'its dangerous craft of picking phrases out from languages that want the living voice', but that applies to the writing of Latin verses rather than to the study of classical authors, and, anyhow, it states only one side of the case. For if these models encourage at times a conventional diction and an artificial attitude to the subject, they teach also neatness and concision of phrasing, and often that limpidity of style which was Wordsworth's own ultimate ideal. Even in Virgil, side by side with the 'elaborately ornate', Wordsworth noted later the 'majestically plain and touching'.[1] Something of what the seventeenth-century lyrists, under the tutelage of rare Ben Jonson, learned from the classics, Wordsworth imbibed in his school-days, an antidote to those vicious tendencies of his own time, to which what he calls his 'outward taste' was too prone to succumb. Thus in the following lines,[2] headed *sunt lacrymae rerum*, in which he adapts the famous Sparrow of Catullus to a Christian sentiment, he shows, together with some poetic feeling, that simplicity of style which fashion was to lead him for a time to discard:

> Pity mourns in plaintive tone
> The lovely starling dead and gone.
> Weep, ye Loves, and Venus, weep
> The lovely starling fallen asleep.
> Venus see with tearful eyes,
> In her lap the starling lies,
> While the Loves all in a ring
> Softly stroke the stiffened wing.

'Stiffened wing', as Polonius would say, is good. Two pages, which must have contained about 20 lines, are

---

[1] *v.* Letter to Lord Lonsdale, 17 February 1819.
[2] This poem, found in one of Coleridge's commonplace books, was included as his composition in his *Literary Remains*, 1836. *v.* Dykes Campbell, *Coleridge's Poetical Works*, pp. 29 and 569; and E. H. Coleridge, *Coleridge's Poems*, pp. 61 and 62.

here torn from the note-book, and the poem closes with
an address to the dead bird:

> Yet art thou happier far than she
> Who felt a mother's love for thee.
> For while her days are days of weeping,
> Thou, in peace, in silence sleeping
> In some still world, unknown, remote[1]
> The mighty Parent's care hast found,
> Without whose tender guardian thought
> No Sparrow falleth to the ground.

In the same school note-book is an imitation of Anacreon, and another early manuscript preserves the
episode of Orpheus and Eurydice translated from the
Georgics; indeed, the manuscripts of the next ten years
bear constant witness to a love of classical authors and
a persistent study of them, which counted for more in
his poetic education than has ever been admitted.

Other schoolboy verses manifest the diversity of his
English reading, and his readiness to play the sedulous
ape to many different poetic modes. A feeble ballad on
a maid of Esthwaite deserted by her lover suggests his
acquaintance with the recent ballad revival; a song
imitative of Chatterton's dirge *My love is dedde* shows
him already beneath the spell of that

> marvellous boy,
> The sleepless soul who perished in his pride;

a conventional sonnet put into the mouth of Mr. ——
on the death of his wife expresses appropriately all the
sentiments appropriate for the occasion, and suggests
that he was fully conversant with the popular sentimental verse of the day, best associated, perhaps, with
the names of Elizabeth Carter, Charlotte Smith, and
Helen Maria Williams. You may remember that a

---

[1] *remote ... thought*: The rhyme is interesting, as illustrating Wordsworth's broad north-country pronunciation; the same rhyme appears
in several places in these early verses. And cf. a letter written by W.
in Sept. 1792, in which, writing rapidly, he spells 'note', 'nought'.

sonnet on seeing Miss Williams weep was the first of
his poems to be printed—it appeared in the *European
Magazine* during his last year at school:

> She wept.—Life's purple tide began to flow
> In languid streams through every thrilling vein.
> Dim were my swimming eyes, my pulse beat slow,
> And my full heart was swell'd to dear delicious pain;

and so on. Wordsworth did not reprint this touching
tribute to Miss Williams's sensibility and his own. And
whether his visit to her, some thirty years later, pro-
voked a recurrence of the 'dear delicious pain', history
does not record.

But his boyhood had other and sterner models, witness a short Idyllium, written to bewail the drowning
of his dog. It is headed by a Latin tag, *Quidquid est
hominum venustiorum, lugete,* and opens not unfamiliarly:

> Where were ye, nymphs, when the remorseless deep
> Clos'd o'er your little favourite's hapless head?
> For neither did ye mark with solemn dream
> In Derwent's rocky woods the white moonbeam
> Pace like a Druid o'er the haunted steep;
> Nor in Winander's stream.

(note the short line). Despite its absurdity this Idyllium
is not without touches of poetic feeling, as in the simile
of the moonbeam, or this, farther on, of the Naiades,

> Your faces white, your tresses green,
> Like waterlilies floating on the tide.

The Druid, doubtless, owes his presence here to Milton's

> steep
> Where your old bards, the famous Druids lie,

but he is not a mere literary reminiscence. The boy
must have known some of the reputed British remains
in his native district, for the Druids haunted his young
imagination, so that his pilgrimage to Stonehenge in
1793, and his emotions there, so eloquently depicted in

The Prelude, were but the climax of an experience that dates from childhood.

His favourite metre at this time was the octosyllabic. This measure had been widely adopted from *Il Penseroso* by the eighteenth-century naturalists, and with them of all his immediate predecessors the young Lakeland poet would obviously feel most affinity. In octosyllabics he wrote his first love poems, of which I shall speak later, and in the same metre he composed *The Vale of Esthwaite*, the most ambitious work of his boyhood. He has told us that it contained many hundred lines; and several hundred of them, clearly but a part of the whole, are preserved on some loose sheets and in two tattered note-books of which many pages are lost. It is a desultory poem, such as he would later have described, not inaptly, as an 'effusion'—not consecutive in thought, with incomplete lines and alternative readings not fitted into the main text. If a fair copy was ever made, none now exists. But even in its rough fragmentary form the poem has a high value, as representing a definite stage in his mental and poetic growth.

As one would expect, its prevalent tone, like that of his models, inclines to morbidity. In *The Recluse* he has referred to

> such damp and gloom
> Of the gay mind as oft splenetic youth
> Mistakes for sorrow,

and elsewhere to

> that sweet and tender melancholy
> Which may itself be cherished and caressed
> More than enough, a fault so natural
> Even with the young, the hopeful, and the gay;

and we have 'more than enough' of it here—not because the boy was not, on the whole, both hopeful and gay, still less because he was posing, but rather because the growing-pains of youth find metrical expression more easily, and somehow seem more poetical, than its exuberance. Moreover the Pleasures of Melancholy, though they were fashionable, had also some basis in fact: 'the deep power of joy', poetically and as well as spiritually, was to be the great discovery of his manhood. Hence, though, under the influence of *L'Allegro*, he 'bids sorrow avaunt', the spirit of *Il Penseroso* soon obtrudes, accompanied by trite moral reflections and tender appeals to pity, in the easy sentimental manner then in vogue.

Akin to this melancholy, and characteristic alike of his own mental state and of the poetic movement of the day, was his association of the terrible and sublime in nature with the mysterious and 'horrid' elements in the romantic tales, the *Arabian Nights*, and other oriental or western legends, on which his youth had fed. The cult for Gothic horror was already in full swing. Percy's translations of Norse poetry had been hailed as a 'mine of wild yet terrific mythology', Hayley, mildest of versifiers, had spoken of 'the Gothic harp's terrific fire'; Bishop Hurd, in his *Essays on Chivalry and Romance*, had asked whether 'there may not be something in the Gothic romance peculiarly suited to the views of genius and of the ends of poetry'. If Hurd's learned discourses had not reached the Hawkshead schoolboy, it is at least probable that he was familiar with Mrs. Barbauld's essay *On the pleasure derived from objects of terror*,[1] in which she maintains that 'the old Gothic Romance and Eastern Tale, however a refined critic may censure them as absurd and extravagant, will ever retain a most powerful influence on the mind', and she calls to witness the 'enchantments drear' that had beguiled the youth of Milton. It was a pleasure

[1] Published in *Miscellaneous Pieces in Prose* by J. and L. Aiken, 1773. The essay is followed by a fragmentary attempt at a tale of romantic horror, *Sir Bertrand*, which contains details remarkably similar to some found in *The Vale of Esthwaite*.

in which the young Wordsworth freely indulged. A favourite poem of his was Beattie's *Minstrel* and, as we know, his sister wrote to a friend that the character of Edwin, its hero, 'resembles much what William was when I first knew him', i.e. just after *The Vale of Esthwaite* was written. And what do we read of Edwin?

> Young Edwin, lighted by the evening star,
> Lingering and listening, wandered down the vale,
> There would he dream of graves, and corses pale,
> And ghosts that to the charnel dungeon throng
> And drag a length of clanking chain, and wail,
> Till silenced by the owl's terrific song
> Or blast that shrieks by fits the shuddering isles among.

Such, apparently, was young William. It seems a retrograde step from the terrible ecstasy of those vaguer emotions which had haunted his earlier childhood, when he hung above the raven's nest, or listened to sounds that are

> The ghostly language of the ancient earth
> Or make their dim abode in distant winds;

and yet he recognized later that this was a natural stage in his mental growth. He saw that romance itself had first arisen, and had lately been revived, to express those 'dumb yearnings and hidden appetites' which must perforce be fed; and when he strove to give voice to his emotions among the sublime and terrible forms of nature, he slipped almost inevitably into the conventional way of expressing them, gave the rein to 'the wilfulness of fancy and conceit', and took over the stock in trade of Gothic romance.

> At noon I hied to gloomy glades
> Religious woods and midnight shades,
> Where brooding Superstition frown'd
> A chill and awful horror round.
>
> .   .   .   .
>
> I loved to haunt the giddy steep
> That hung loose-trembling o'er the deep,

> While ghosts of Murtherers mounted fast
> And grimly glar'd upon the blast,
> While the dark whirlwind, rob'd unseen
> With black arm rear'd the clouds between
>
> .   .   .   .
>
> While, her dark cheek all ghastly bright,
> Like a chained Madman laugh'd the Night.

And the following might be described as Mrs. Radcliffe in octosyllabics, though Mrs. Radcliffe had not yet written:

> Now did I love the dismal gloom
> Of haunted castle's panell'd room,
> Listening the wild wind's wailing song
> Whistling the rattling doors among;
> When as I heard a rustling sound
> My haggard eyes would turn around,
> Which straight a female form survey'd,
> Tall, and in silken vest array'd.
> Her face of pale and ashy hue
> And in one hand a taper blue;
> As at the door she seem'd to stand
> And beckoning slowly wav'd her hand
> I rose, above my head a bell
> The mansion shook with solemn knell.
> Through . . . green damp windings dark and steep,
> She brought me to a dungeon deep,
> Then stopped, and thrice her hand she shook,
> More pale and ghastly seemed her look.
> The taper turned from blue to red,
> Flash'd out, and with a shriek she fled.
> With arms in horror spread around
> I mov'd, a form unseen I found
> Twist round my hand an icy chain
>   And drag me to the spot again.

All this would be forgivable in a mere romantic schoolboy, caught in the toils of literary fashion; but Wordsworth was too much a child of the eighteenth century to outgrow it with his unrazored youth. It persisted, indeed, right on into his early manhood. Some years later, the exact date not determinable, he perpetrated a romantic narrative in pseudo-Spenserian stanzas. On a wild tempestuous night a youth guides a blind old man and his dog over rough precipitous ground to a ruined castle, and together they take refuge in its dungeon underground. The old man is pitifully grateful to his guide, who, however, is all the while meditating his murder. But before he can do the deed, he is checked by several typically Gothic portents—two sinister figures bearing a white burden, and a third with spade and crow-bar, then a grim phantom, and a hand of fleshly hue; and when, not to be denied, he lifts his murderous aim, a rumbling noise is heard, passing into a sound of uncouth horror, which is echoed by a rending peal of fearful and mysterious import. The noise awakens his would-be victim, and here the fragment breaks off. The lines are spirited, and would do credit to any contemporary purveyor of romantic terror. For us they have a twofold interest. First, we recognize in the main incident a foreshadowing of the central scene in *The Borderers*; secondly, in the description of the ruined castle, which is quite well done in the conventional Gothic manner, we are suddenly startled by meeting with a familiar and characteristically Wordsworthian line:

> So saying, by the hand he led his charge
> On through the passage of the ponderous keep,
> That opened to a court of circuit large
> Whose walls had scattered many a stony heap.
> The unimaginable touch of time
> Or shouldering rend had split with ravin deep
> The towers that stately stood, as in their prime.

More than a quarter of a century later one line from this welter of Gothic absurdity returned, to put the last perfect touch on a superb sonnet, wherein the poet describes

the tower
Of yesterday, which royally did wear
His crown of weeds, but could not even sustain
Some casual shout that broke the silent air,
Or the unimaginable touch of Time.

As this tale is a fragment we cannot tell whether it had
any other aim than to curdle the blood; but the first
draft of *Guilt of Sorrow*,[1] *or an Incident on Salisbury*

---

[1] Some of this supernatural horror persists in the published version,
and it was probably the difficulty of purging the poem of it entirely
that led him to think poorly of the work and consign it to his *Juvenilia*.
The early manuscript version contains still more of this 'horror'. Thus
when the sailor reaches Stonehenge,

> A voice as from a tomb in hollow accents cried:

> 'Oh from that mountain pile avert thy face
> Whate'er betide at this tremendous hour
> To hell's most cursed sprites the baleful place
> Belongs, uprearèd by their magic power;
> Though mixed with flame rush down the crazing shower,
> And o'er thy naked bed the thunders roll,
> Fly ere at once the fiends their prey devour,
> Or grinning, on thy endless tortures scowl,
> Till very madness seem a mercy to thy soul.

> 'For oft, at dead of night, when dreadful fire
> Unfolds that powerful circle's reddening stones,
> Mid priests and spectres grim and idols dire
> Far heard the great flame utters human moans;
> Then all is hushed; again the desert groans,
> A dismal light its farthest bounds illumes.
> While warrior spectres of gigantic bones
> Forth-issuing from a thousand rifted tombs
> Wheel on their fiery steeds amid the infernal glooms.'

> He heard no more,

and, indeed, one might admit that he had already heard enough.
Fleeing, he reaches a lonely spital where he 'thinks himself to rest':

> Ah me! that last of hopes is fled apace,
> For, entering in, his hair in horror rose
> To hear a voice that seemed to mourn in sorrow's throes.

He discovers that the voice proceeds from a poor woman who, like him,
is sheltering from the storm, and his hair subsides, but only to rise

Plain (1793–4), had, we know, a passionately humanitarian purpose; yet it is marred by a similarly crude supernaturalism, quite out of keeping with its essential spirit, nor is the tragedy of *The Borderers* free from the same un-Wordsworthian taint. So hardly did he shake off this baleful influence upon his youth.

But we must return to the *Vale of Esthwaite*, for I would not leave the impression that it is a mere sequence of follies slowly to be outgrown: it gives, indeed, a true foretaste of what was to come. Despite these incursions into the realm of horrid phantasy the boy had, too, a real world about him, and in the delicacy of his perceptions he was already something of himself. Thus he

> Marks the white smoke, rising slow
> From the wood-built pile below,
> Rise like a spirit on its way,
> Hang lingering round with fond delay;

or notes, at evening, how

> The ploughboy by his jingling wain
> Whistles along the ringing lane,
> And as he strikes with sportive lash
> The leaves of the o'erhanging ash,
> Wavering they fall; while at the sound
> The blinking bats flit round and round.

In a note dictated to Miss Fenwick in 1843 Wordsworth remarked that thoughts and images from *The Vale of Esthwaite* are dispersed among his later writings. The images recur, not because he had recourse to the old manuscript and worked it up to suit his present purpose, but rather because, from early childhood, his mind was, as he says, impressed with forms 'that yet exist with independent life', so that ever and anon they rose before his consciousness. Thus in *An Evening Walk* we find the 'bat-haunted ash', and another of the vivid images

again as she recounts, in several lurid stanzas, the supernatural horrors of the place.

in that poem, 'the tremulous sob of the complaining owl', looks back to

> The moaning owl shall soon
> Sob long and tremulous to the moon

of *The Vale of Esthwaite*, just as it looks forward to the owlets that charm the Idiot Boy on that magical moon-lit night, as

> They lengthen out the tremulous sob
> That echoes far from hill to hill.

On a couplet from *An Evening Walk*:

> And fronting the bright West, yon oak entwines
> Its darkening boughs and leaves in stronger lines,

Wordsworth wrote the significant comment: 'This is feebly and imperfectly expressed, but I recollect distinctly the very spot where this first struck me. . . . The moment was important in my poetical history, for I date from it my consciousness of the infinite variety of natural appearances which had been unnoticed by the poets of any age or country, in so far as I was acquainted with them, and I made a resolution to supply in some degree the deficiency.' In the fulfilment of this resolve lies a part of his great achievement as a poet, and, as a schoolboy, he had already begun to achieve it. Thus the couplet I have just quoted is foreshadowed in *The Vale of Esthwaite*:

> Now while the dazzling glare of day
> Fades, slowly fades, from gold to grey,
> The oak its boughs and foliage twines
> Mark'd to the view in stronger lines,
> While, every darkening leaf between,
> The sky distinct and clear is seen.

But the images have a deeper significance and a stronger power of survival when they are associated with some specially poignant feeling. No reader of *The Prelude* can forget the vision the poet saw as a child, of a shepherd on the hillside, upon a day of alter-

nate mist and sunshine, when his love for Nature awoke
in him a conscious love of human kind:

> Along a narrow Valley and profound
> I journey'd, when aloft above my head,
> Emerging from the silvery vapours, lo!
> A Shepherd and his Dog! in open day:
> Girt round with mists they stood and look'd about
> From that enclosure small, inhabitants
> Of an aerial Island floating on,
> A little pendant area of grey rocks
> By the soft wind breath'd forward;[1]

Here is the schoolboy version of the same incident:

> And see, the mist, as warms the day
> From the green vale steals away;
> Yet round the mountain top it sails
> Slow borne upon the dewy gales;
> And on yon summit brown and bare
> That seems an island in the air,
> The shepherd's restless dog I mark,
> Who bounding round with frequent bark
> Now leaps around the uncovered plain,
> Now dives into the mist again,
> And while the guiding sound he hears
> The [   ] shepherd lad appears
> And clasps his clinging dog for joy.

And you all remember that 'spot of time', as he calls it
in *The Prelude*, when, just before his father's death, he
waited by the whistling hawthorn tree, and the wall
that sheltered the sheep from the storm, for the horses
that were to take him and his brothers home for the
holidays:

> One Evening when the wintry blast
> Through the sharp Hawthorn whistling pass'd,
> And the poor flocks all pinch'd with cold
> Sad-drooping sought the mountain fold,
> Long, long, upon yon naked rock
> Alone, alone, I bore the shock;

[1] *v. The Prelude* (1805), viii. 92–101.

Long, long, my swimming eyes did roam
For little Horse to bear me home,
To bear me,[1]—what avails my tear?
To sorrow o'er a Father's bier.
Flow on, in vain thou hast not flow'd
But eased me of a heavy load;
For much it gives my heart relief
To pay the nightly debt of grief;
With sighs repeated o'er and o'er
I mourn because I mourned no more.
Nor did my little heart foresee
She lost a home in losing thee,
Nor did she know, of thee bereft,
That little more than Heaven was left.[2]

After this the poem tails off into tame and puerile reflections. 'A still voice whispers to [his] breast' that he 'soon shall be with them that rest' and in a vein of vapid sentimentalism he begs some kind and pious friend to pay his grave 'the tribute of a tear'. Thus he is led on to apostrophize the 'friend of his soul' who surely will never forget him; then, cheering up a little, it occurs to him that after all he may have a long life before him, and he concludes with the conviction that wherever fate may lead him he will always cast a longing, lingering look back upon his 'Dear Native Regions'.

[1] *To bear me*: The most noticeable stylistic trick of W.'s early poems is the continued use of repetition, partly, perhaps, caught from Spenser, partly due to a tentative feeling after his subject as he writes.

[2] Another interesting anticipation of *The Prelude* is found in a fragment of a poem to his dog, written in his school-days, but probably not a part of *The Vale of Esthwaite*, as the rhymes are not in couplets.

> If, while I gazed, to Nature blind,
> On the calm ocean of my mind,
> Some new created Image rose
> In full grown Beauty at its birth,
> Lovely as Venus from the sea,
> Then, while my glad hand sprung to thee,
> We were the happiest pair on earth.

Cf. *The Prelude*, iv. 111–17.

The Vale of Esthwaite was completed in the early summer of 1787,[1] just before he left school. His holidays were passed at Penrith, and here he rejoined the playmate of his childhood, from whom he had been parted since their mother's death nine years before. Dorothy's impressions of her newly recovered brother are recorded in her letters: William's feelings on their reunion we now hear from his own lips. For opposite those lines in which he had lamented that with the loss of his father and his home 'little more than Heaven was left', he now wrote:

> Sister, for whom I feel a love
> Which warms a Brother far above,
> On you, as sad she marks the scene,
> Why does my heart so fondly lean?
> Why, but because to you is given
> All, all my soul could wish from Heaven?
> Why, but because I fondly view
> All, all that heaven has claimed, in you?

[1] The respective dates of the *Poems written in Youth*, as found in the various editions of W., and based for the most part on statements made by him in old age, are often incorrect and misleading. Thus 'Dear native regions' (the close of *The Vale of E.*) is dated 1786, but one of the manuscripts clearly states that the poem was written in the spring and summer of 1787. Moreover 'Dear native regions' has been much altered from its form in the manuscript and hence in either case does not truly represent what W. wrote in his boyhood. Similarly 'Calm is all nature' is said to have been composed in 1786, and the *Lines written while sailing in a boat* and *Remembrance of Collins* (printed as one poem in 1798) are dated 1789; but a manuscript note-book used at Racedown shows that he was still at work on them in 1795-7. *Lines left upon a seat in a Yew Tree* is said to have been begun in 1787 and completed in 1795, but it is very doubtful whether much of it was written as early as 1787, and almost certain that none of it was then in blank verse, whilst it was not finished before the early months of 1797, when Mary Hutchinson was at Racedown, and copied it into a note-book. Of *An Evening Walk* the date is said to be 1787, but it is well-nigh certain that W. was not at work on it simultaneously with *The Vale of E.* He probably only gave it the date 1787 because, in it, he worked up several passages from *The Vale of E. An Evening Walk* is really the work of his first two long vacations, 1788 and 1789.

Here is the first halting utterance of a devotion that was to endure for more than sixty years, and was destined to inspire verse as lovely as poet ever lavished upon his mistress.

Henceforth Dorothy was to be a close partner in his poetic life. From Cambridge he seems to have sent her most of what he wrote, and to her he dedicated *An Evening Walk*, his first bid for poetic fame, composed during his first two long vacations. He now discarded the octosyllabic in favour of the more formal heroic couplet, and with that measure took over all the stylistic vices of its latest exponents, overgoing them in preciosity of language, in meaningless personification of the abstract, in harsh transference of epithets and forced constructions; so that, despite its vivid and truthful perception, it offers an extreme example of that false poetic diction against which he was later to tilt. And the faults of *An Evening Walk* were exaggerated in *Descriptive Sketches*, which he wrote in 1792. But the style of *The Female Vagrant*, begun at the same time, makes it clear that he had only been led thus far astray by a youthful subservience to fashion: for in that poem written in Spenserian stanzas, the language and constructions are, on the whole, simple and straightforward. As Coleridge remarked of it,[1] 'the occasional obscurities [of the *Descriptive Sketches*] had almost wholly disappeared, together with that worse defect of arbitrary and illogical phrases, at once hackneyed and fantastic'.

The earliest version of *Guilt and Sorrow*,[2] or an *Incident on Salisbury Plain*, of which *The Female Vagrant* is a part, is preserved in a note-book dating from 1794,

[1] *v. Biog. Lit.* chap. iv. Coleridge speaks there of a poem which 'still remains unpublished [1817], but of which the stanza, and tone of style, were the same as those of *The Female Vagrant*'. But he was almost certainly thinking, not of a separate poem, but of that part of *Guilt and Sorrow* which was not published in 1798.

[2] The early manuscript of the poem is headed simply *A night on Salisbury Plain*.

when the poet, after three years' separation, was again
reunited to his sister; and at Windy Brow, near Keswick,
they housed together for the first time. A poem on
Harmodius and Aristogeiton, and a translation of
Horace's *Fons Bandusiae*, show that he is still keeping
up his classics; of deeper interest, both poetic and bio-
graphical, is a poem headed *Septimi Gades*, and modelled
on the sixth Ode of Horace's Second Book.[1] Just as
Horace voices a longing for a 'kind and calm retreat' at
Tibur, or, failing that, by the stream of Galesus, than
which, he says, 'no spot so joyous smiles to me', and
then assures his friend Septimius,

> That happy place, that sweet retreat,
> The charming hills that round it rise,
> Your latest hours and mine await;

so Wordsworth invites his love to join him, if not in
some valley of the Rhône, such as he had visited on his
Alpine tour, then at Grasmere. But the lady whom he
invites is not, as some would expect, Annette Vallon: it
is Mary Hutchinson.

> Oh thou, whose fixed bewildered eye,
> In strange and dreary vacancy
> Of tenderness severe,
> With fear unnamed my bosom chilled,
> While thus thy farewell accents thrilled,
> Or seemed to thrill my ear;
>
> Think not, my friend, from me to roam,
> Thy arms shall be my only home,
> My only bed thy breast;
> No separate path our lives shall know,
> But where thou goest I shall go,
> And there my bones shall rest.

[1] I quote from the translation of Philip Francis (1743) which Dr.
Johnson thought the best; it was probably known to Wordsworth in
Anderson's Collection.

Oh! might we seek that humble shed
Which sheltered once my pilgrim head,
Where, down the mountains thrown,
A streamlet seeks, through forest glooms,
Through viny glades and orchard blooms,
Below, the solemn Rhone.

But if the wayward fates deny
Those purple slopes, that azure sky,
My willing voice shall hail
The lone grey cots and pastoral steeps,
That shine inverted in the deeps
Of Grasmere's quiet vale.

To him who faint and heartless stands
On pale Arabia's thirsty sands,
How fair that fountain seems
Where last, beneath the palmy shade
In bowers of rose and jasmine laid,
He quaffed the living streams.

As fair in Memory's eye appear,
Sweet scene of peace, thy waters clear
Thy turf and folding groves;
On gales perfumed by every flower
Of mountain top or mead or bower
Thy honey people roves.

What finny myriads twinkle bright
Along thy streams—how pure and white
The flocks thy shepherds fold;
What brimming pails thy milkmaids bear,
Nor wants the jolly Autumn there
His crown of waving gold.

Yes, Nature on those vivid meads,
Those [1] slopes and mountain heads,
Has showered her various wealth;
There Temperance and Truth abide
And Toil with Leisure at his side,
And Chearfulness and Health.

1 *Those* [   ] *slopes*: The manuscript has a blank space here.

No spot does parting Phoebus greet
With farewell smile more fond and sweet
Than those sequestered hills;
While, as composing shades invest
With purple gloom the water's breast,
The grove its music stills.

When shouts and sheepfold bells and sound
Of flocks and herds and streams rebound
Along the ringing dale,
How beauteous, round that gleaming tide,
The silvery morning vapours glide,
And half the landscape veil.

Methinks that morning scene displays
A lovely emblem of our days,
Unobvious and serene;
So shall our still lives, half betrayed,
Shew charms more touching from their shade,
Though veiled, yet not unseen.

Yes, Mary, to some lowly door
In that delicious spot obscure
Our happy feet shall tend;
And there for many a golden year
Fair Hope shall steal thy voice, to chear
Thy poet and thy friend.

Though loudly roar the wintry flood
And Tempest shake the midnight wood
And rock our little nest;
Love with his tenderest kiss shall dry
Thy human tear and still the sigh
That heaves thy gentle breast.

It seems, indeed, that, though for a time his passion for
Annette had swept him off his feet, a year's absence had
cooled his ardour, and brought him back to his old love.
For that Mary was *that* we know from a line in a draft of
The Prelude where she is spoken of as 'the maid to whom
were breathed my first fond vows', and the statement
finds further support in the verses of his school-days.

He had known Mary from childhood, at the Penrith
dame school they had learned to read out of the same
book, and at Penrith, where Mary lived, he had spent
his school holidays since his father died. It was on
returning to school in August 1786 that his first love
poems were written, and when they mention the lady's
name the name is Mary, whilst such descriptions of her
as are given fit in with what we know of Mary's appearance and character. She is dark-haired, her eyes soft
and sleepy, her forehead smooth and clear, her temper
sober and quiet rather than excitable and passionate:

> High o'er the silver rocks I roved
> To wander from the form I loved,
> In hope fond Fancy would be kind
> And steal my Mary from my mind;[1]

so he writes, but, do what he can, he cannot forget her.
In the same month he penned an imitation of Anacreon,[2]
to which I have already referred. As Anacreon had
invoked the best of painters to portray for him 'the
pasture land of lovers', so this love-lorn schoolboy calls
on Sir Joshua Reynolds to paint him a portrait of his
sweetheart. The best passage in his ode bears a striking
resemblance in idea and imagery to the conclusion of
Septimi Gades:

> Loosely chaste o'er all below
> Let the snowy mantle flow,
> As silvered by the morning beam
> The white mist curls[3] on Grasmere's stream,
> Which, like a veil of flowing light,
> Hides half the landskip from the sight.

[1] For the whole poem *v*. E. de S., *Wordsworth's Poetical Works*,
vol. i, p. 263, *Beauty and Moonlight, An Ode*, which Coleridge re-
fashioned into *Lewti*, first published in the *Morning Post*, 13 April 1798,
and included in *Sibylline Leaves*, 1817. *v*. E. H. Coleridge, *Coleridge's
Poems*, pp. 253 and 1049-52.

[2] *imitation of Anacreon*: i.e. the Ode beginning Ἄγε ζωγράφων
ἄριστε.

[3] For note 3 see next page.

Here I see the wandering rill,
The white flocks sleeping on the hill,
While Fancy paints, beneath the veil,
The pathway winding through the dale,
The cot, the seat of Peace and Love,
Peeping through the tufted grove.

Notice how many of the same images occur in both poems—the gleaming water, the silvery morning vapour hiding half the landscape, the pastoral slopes, the lowly cot obscure—an emblem, in its sheltered seclusion, of the life that awaits them there. It is hard to doubt that the same maiden[1] is addressed in the two poems. And just as they both point to an early attachment to Mary, so do they emphasize the early hold that Grasmere, of all spots on earth, had laid upon his heart. In *The Recluse* he has told how a schoolboy jaunt took him to Grasmere, and its loveliness so smote him that he felt this to be the one place where he would fain live and die. It was at Grasmere, too, that he first saw the mist curling over the lake, it was on Dunmail Raise, just above Grasmere, that he first saw the shepherd striding through the mist, and love for humanity was

[3] *The white mist curls*: Cf. also *The Prelude* (1805), i. 589–92.

> A Child, I held unconscious intercourse
> With the eternal Beauty, drinking in
> A pure organic pleasure from the lines
> Of curling mist . . .

The version of 1850 reads:

> Organic pleasure from the silver wreaths, &c.

Cf. also *To May* (1826–34), Oxf. W. 508.

> Such gentle mists as glide
> Curling with unconfirmed intent
> On that green mountain's side.

[1] It is worth noting, too, that in *The Prelude*, vi. 14, where he recounts his return to Cambridge after that long vacation most of which had been spent at Hawkshead in Lancashire, it is not to the maids of *Hawkshead* that he bids adieu but to the 'frank-hearted maids of Cumberland', i.e. of Penrith, where Mary lived.

awakened in him. On his way to Windy Brow with Dorothy he spent a night there, and when he settled down to correct and add to *An Evening Walk*, one of the first passages he added described the village green where his own children were afterwards to play, and later to be laid to rest:

> I seek that footworn spot of level ground
> Close by the school within the churchyard's bound,
> Through every race of them who near are laid
> For children's sports kept sacred from the spade;
> Such the smooth spot that skirts the mouldering rows
> Of graves where Grasmere's rustic sons repose;
> From seats on the side wall the agèd bend
> And elms above their rugged arms extend.
> What tribes of happy youth have gambolled here,
> Nor in their wild mirth ever thought how near
> Their sensible warm motion[1] was allied
> To the dull clod that crumbles at their side.

Thus it was for Wordsworth with places as with persons. It is eminently characteristic of the poet, for whom 'the child was father of the man', that those feelings which in the end proved deepest and most permanent should be found rooted and grounded in the experiences of boyhood.

His chief business at Windy Brow was the revision of *An Evening Walk*. Most of the alterations found in the edition of 1842 were made at Windy Brow in 1794, so that the second version, hardly less than the first, represents early work. But he did not merely alter, he now added much that has never seen the light. One of

---

[1] *Sensible warm motion*: from the famous speech of Claudio in *Measure for Measure* (III. i. 120) when he was condemned to death for adultery. The play was evidently in Wordsworth's mind at the time, for two lines in the *Incident on Salisbury Plain* are corrected to

> Their sensible warm motions transport swayed
> By day, and Peace at night her cheek between them laid.

I present this note to those who are still suffering from the Annette complex.

these additions I have just quoted: I shall give you
another, which illustrates the growth of that humaner
sentiment, extending from man to the animal creation,
that was consequent on his experiences in France, and
the awakening in him of that sense of life in Nature,
which characterizes his maturer work. To the description of Rydal Falls he now added the reference to
Horace's *Fons Bandusiae*, which he had just translated,
and after the passage, printed in 1842, which deprecates
the sacrifice of an innocent kid—such lovely scenes, he
avers, should be approached with

> A mind . . . in a calm angelic mood
> Of happy wisdom, meditating love,—

the manuscript goes on:

> A heart that vibrates, evermore awake
> To feeling for all forms that Life can take,
> That wider still its sympathy extends
> And sees not any line where being ends,
> Sees sense through Nature's rudest forms betrayed,
> Tremble obscure in fountain, rock, and shade,
> And while a secret power those forms endears
> Their social accents never vainly hears.

Here is a germ of the faith that was to inspire the
Lines written in early Spring and *Hartleap Well*.

And the early version of *Guilt and Sorrow*, which he
was writing in the previous year and was now copied
out by Dorothy, contains unprinted stanzas which show
him keenly alive to the misery and wrong that oppress
the world both at home and abroad, and oppress our
own distracted times no less than his. These days may
be better, he writes, than those when superstition was
rife, and the Druids exacted their toll of human sacrifice; yet, even now, what does the light of reason
achieve for us, save to

> Reveal with still-born glimpse the terrors of our day?
> For proof, if man thou lovest, turn thine eye
> On realms which least the cup of Misery taste;

For want how many men and Children die;
How many, at Oppression's portal placed
Receive the scanty dole she cannot waste;
And bless, as she has taught, the hand benign.
How many, by inhuman toil debased,
Abject, obscure and brute, to earth incline
Unrespited, forlorn of every spark divine!

Nor only is the walk of private life
Unblessed by Justice and the kindly train
Of Peace and truth, while Injury and strife
Outrage and deadly Hate usurp their reign.
From the pale line to either frozen main
The nations, forced at home in bonds to drink
The dregs of Wretchedness, for empire strain;
And when by their own fetters crushed they sink
Move their galled limbs in fear, and eye each silent link.

.   .   .   .

And then, after a few lost stanzas that must have put
up a defence for the existing state of things, he goes on:

How weak the solace such fond thoughts afford
When with untimely stroke the virtuous bleed.
Say, rulers of the nations, from the sword
Can aught but murder, pain, and tears proceed?
Oh, what can war but endless war still breed?
Or whence but from the labours of the sage
Can poor benighted mortals gain the meed
Of happiness and virtue, how assuage
But by his gentle words their self-consuming rage?

Insensate they who think, at wisdom's porch,
That Exile, Terror, Bonds and Force may stand;
That Truth with human blood can feed his torch,
And Justice balance with her gory hand
Scales whose dire weight of human heads demand
A Nero's arm. Must Law with its own scourge
Still torture crimes that grew a monstrous band
Formed by his care, and still his victims urge
With voice that breathes despair to death's tremendous verge?

.   .   .   .

Heroes of Truth, pursue your march, uptear
The oppressors' dungeon from its deepest base;
High o'er the towers of Pride undaunted rear
Resistless in your might th' Herculean mace
Of Reason, let foul Error's monstrous race
Dragged from their dens start at the light with pain
And die! pursue your toils till not a trace
Be left on earth of Superstition's reign
Save that eternal pile which frowns on Sarum's plain.

In its wide humanitarianism, its passion for justice,
its conviction that crime is largely the inevitable outcome of social conditions, its sublime faith in the power
of Reason to inaugurate an earthly Utopia, these stanzas
reveal the poet at the height of his early Godwinian
enthusiasm, when his faith in the Revolution was still
undimmed. But within the next year came a great
revulsion. France failed him, and in his distress God-
winism proved a rotten prop. This was his 'soul's last
and lowest ebb', and only gradually, in the quiet of
Racedown, under his sister's ministrations, aided later
by the stimulus of Coleridge, did he regain his peace of
mind. The poetry of the time reflects his mental state.
His first occupation was to make alterations and additions to *Salisbury Plain*, so that 'it can be looked upon
as almost another work', and it is significant that the
confident appeal to Heroes of Truth in the last stanza
of the poem is now cut out. Next he busied himself
with Juvenalian satire on the corruption in high places,
and this was followed by his tragedy of *The Borderers*,
in which, though he exposes the fallacies of Godwin,
he has found no satisfying creed to take its place.
Lastly he wrote the first draft of the *Ruined Cottage*,
but without that setting, added a little later, which
puts the tragedy into a sane perspective. There is also
a fragment, relating in words of more passionate disapproval than in *The Prelude*, how at the Isle of Wight,

in the summer of 1794, he had heard the guns of the
fleet about to set sail for France:

> But hark! from yon proud fleet[1] in peal profound
> Thunders the sunset cannon; at the sound
> The star of life appears to set in blood,
> And Ocean shudders in offended mood,
> Deepening with moral gloom his angry flood.

Only at the close of the *Lines left upon a Seat in a Yew-
tree*, with its warnings against the dangers of morbid
introspection and self-sufficiency, does the authentic
Wordsworth emerge:

> True knowledge leads to love;
> True dignity abides with him alone,
> Who, in the silent hour of inward thought,
> Can still suspect, and still revere himself
> In lowliness of heart.

This poem was completed early in 1797, after many
fumblings, and the same note-book contains several pages
of morbid moralizing, against which he has written, not
without justice, 'mournful stuff'.

But the Racedown manuscripts are not all dreary
reading, they show him also to be steadily advancing in
his art. Rough drafts of *Calm is all Nature* and of lines
written at Richmond, usually dated 1789, prove that
these poems only now reached their published form.
He was continuing his classical experiments; for apart
from the Juvenalian satire there are imitations of one
or two love poems from the Greek; and again he tries
his hand at the romantic ballad. More interesting,
however, is a long fragment of the second part of *The
Three Graves*, of which the third and fourth, written
by Coleridge at Nether Stowey, first appeared in *The
Friend* of 1809. The story, as you remember, is of unnatural, abnormal passion. On the eve of her daughter's
marriage a widowed mother attempts to supplant her

---

[1] *But hark! from yon proud fleet*: Cf. *The Prelude* (1805), x. 291–307.

in her sweetheart's affections, and when he repulses her
with laughter, she curses their wedlock. So far the first
two parts; the third and fourth relate the effects of the
mother's curse on the two lovers and upon the friend
who shared their home. Now when Coleridge printed
The Three Graves[1] he gave the story of the first two
parts in prose, and the questions must often have been
asked why he did this, instead of giving the whole story
in verse, and why, on printing it, he promised, if the
fragment met with favour, to print a fifth and a sixth
part, but still said nothing about the first and second.
The reason that he did not publish the fifth and sixth is,
of course, that, like so much that Coleridge projected,
they were never written; and, indeed, as the fourth
concludes the tale, it is difficult to see what they could
have contained; the reason why he did not publish the

[1] The following extract from Barron Field's unpublished *Memoirs
of the Life and Poetry of W. W.* (B.M. MS. Add. 4135-7), to which
Professor Arthur Beatty has kindly called my attention, is interesting
in this connexion:

'Mr. Wordsworth one day said to me: "It is not enough for a poet
to possess the power of mind; he must also have knowledge of the heart,
and this can only be acquired by time and tranquil silence. No great
poem has been written by a young man or by an unhappy one. It was
poor dear Coleridge's constant infelicity that prevented him from
being the poet that Nature had given him the power to be. He had
always too much personal and domestic discontent to paint the sorrows
of mankind. He could not

afford to suffer
With those whom he saw suffer.

I gave him the subject of his Three Graves; but he made it too shocking
and painful, and not sufficiently sweetened by any healing views. Not
being able to dwell on or sanctify natural woes, he took to the supernatural, and hence his Antient Mariner and Christabel, in which he
shows great poetical power; but these things have not the hold on the
heart which Nature gives, and will never be popular poems, like Gold-
smith's or Burns's." '

It is interesting to speculate how Wordsworth would have 'sweetened'
the subject with 'healing views', if he had completed the poem himself
at some later period.

first and second is now seen to be because he did not
write them. For the manuscript proves conclusively
that the second part, and therefore presumably the
first, as well as the original conception of the poem, are
Wordsworth's. The second part is copied into the
note-book partly by Mary Hutchinson, and we know
that Mary Hutchinson left Racedown before Coleridge
arrived there, moreover alterations in the text in Wordsworth's hand prove it to be his work and not a copy of
another's. The homely style which Coleridge adopted
in the third and fourth parts, for which, indeed, he
apologizes, so different from his normal style, is now
explained, for it was inevitably determined by the style
of the previous parts; and he was probably led to under-
take it, after Wordsworth had thrown it aside, partly
because at that time he had a passionate and not wholly
critical admiration for anything that fell from the lips
or the pen of his new friend, and partly because of its
obvious psychological possibilities. For the story, if
unpleasant, is at least less improbable than the plot of
The Borderers, which Coleridge had just pronounced
to be 'absolutely wonderful'.

Yet we can understand, too, why Wordsworth threw
it aside. He had begun it when the morbid and the
unnatural had still a fascination for him. But the clouds
had lifted, and in the exultation of his recovered faith
in human nature he resolved henceforth to write of
'joy in widest commonalty spread', or, if of sorrow,
then only of

> Sorrow that is not sorrow but delight
> And miserable love that is not pain
> To hear of, for the glory that redounds
> Therefrom to human kind, and what we are.

He had definitely broken with all that was misguided
or melancholy in his past. The hidden appetites and
dumb yearnings of his spirit no longer sought satisfaction

in a false supernaturalism, or Gothic horror, for they
had found their answer in

> something far more deeply interfused,
> Whose dwelling is the light of setting suns,
> And the round ocean and the living air,
> And the blue sky, and in the mind of man.

And for the expression of this new vision of the world
there is no call for a style of false and showy splendour,
for 'Nature is too pure to be refined'. But while he is
thus reacting against the errors of his recent past, he is,
in reality, making a conscious return to the instinctive
faith of his childhood, and discovering at last the true
scope and direction of his essential genius:

> Long have I loved what I behold,
> The night that calms, the day that cheers;
> The common growth of mother earth
> Suffices me—her tears, her mirth,
> Her humblest mirth and tears.

> The dragon's wing, the magic ring,
> I shall not covet for my dower,
> If I along that lowly way
> With sympathetic heart may stray,
> And with a soul of power.

> These given, what more need I desire
> To stir, to soothe, or elevate?
> What nobler marvels than the mind
> May in life's daily prospect find,
> May find or there create?

By his devotion to this purpose he became one of the
greatest and most original of our poets. And if, at
times, his criticism of verse written with other aims
than his own lacked sympathy, and if his attacks on
poetic diction were too sweeping, was it not in part,
perhaps, because he remembered the Delilahs by whom
his own youth had been ensnared?

II

WORDSWORTH AND HIS DAUGHTER'S MARRIAGE[1]

AMONG the stories current of Wordsworth's later life none is, perhaps, more often told, or more often misrepresented, than that of his opposition to the marriage of his daughter, Dora.

'His love for his only daughter', wrote Sir Henry Taylor in his *Autobiography*, 'was passionately jealous, and the marriage which was indispensable to her peace and happiness was intolerable to his feelings. The emotions, I may say the throes and agonies of emotion, he underwent were such as an old man could not have endured without suffering in health, had he not been a very strong old man. But he was like nobody else, old or young. He would pass the night, or most part of it, in struggles and storms, to the moment of coming down to breakfast, and then, if strangers were present, be as easy and delightful in conversation as if nothing was the matter. But if his own health did not suffer, his daughter's did; and this consequence of his resistance, mainly aided, I believe, by the temperate but persistent pressure exercised by Miss Fenwick, brought him at length, though far too tardily, to consent to the marriage.'

This statement is undoubtedly true of Wordsworth's affection for his daughter, and his dislike of her marriage, but it is not the whole truth; for it does not suggest that he had any reason, other than 'passionate jealousy', for his objection; while the careless copying and dating of three of his letters has given to the phrase 'far too tardily' a meaning which is wholly at variance with the facts.

A chatty anonymous article, studded with errors, appeared in the *Cornhill Magazine* of March 1893,

[1] From *Wordsworth and Coleridge: Studies in honor of George McLean Harper*, edited by E. L. Griggs (Princeton University Press, 1939).

under the title 'Some Unpublished Letters of William Wordsworth'. In one of those letters [A], addressed to 'dearest M[ary] and D[ora],' undated, but from its reference to the poem *The Triad* clearly written in 1828, occur these sentences:

'Say to Mr Monkhouse C. Wilson's behaviour shews the good sense of Dr Venables' advice.'

'Have nothing to do with Quillinan. I am sorry for his disappointment. I hope dear Dora's looks are better, and that she will collect some flesh as Edith [Southey] did.'

Then after remarking that Dora's marriage was a severe trial to the poet and his wife, and some inaccurate statements about Quillinan, the article goes on to transcribe two further letters, [B] and [C], again undated.

[B]

Sunday morning, Nine o'clock

My dearest Dora,—I am looking for Mr Quillinan every moment. I hope to revive the conversation of yesterday.

The sum is:—I make no opposition to this marriage. I have no resentment connected with it towards anyone; you know how much friendship I have always felt towards Mr Q. and how much I respect him. I do not doubt the strength of his love and affection towards you: this, as far as I am concerned, is the fair side of the case.

On the other hand, I cannot think of parting with you with that complacency, that satisfaction, that hopefulness which I could wish to feel: there is too much of necessity in the case for my wishes. But I must submit, and do submit, and God Almighty bless you, my dear child, and him who is the object of your long, and long-tried preference and choice.

Ever your affectionate father,

Wm. Wordsworth.

I have said little above of your dear mother, the best of women. O how my heart is yearning towards her, and you, and my poor dear sister.

[C]

Thursday

Your letter to me just received. Thanks: I will write you from Brinsop. W. W.[1]

My dear Daughter,—The letter which you must have received from Wm [i.e. her brother Willy] has placed before you my judgment and feelings: how far you are reconciled to them I am unable to divine. I have only to add that I believe Mr Q. to be a most honorable and upright man, and further, that he is most strongly and faithfully attached to you: this I must solemnly declare in justice to you both; and to this I add *my blessing upon you and him*—more I cannot do, and if this does not content you with what your brother has said, we must all abide by God's decision upon our respective fates. Mr Q. is, I trust, aware how slender my means are; the state of Wm's health will undoubtedly entail upon us considerable expense, and how John[2] is to get on without our aid, I cannot foresee. No more at present, my time is out. I am going to join Miss Fenwick at Miss Pollard's.

Ever your most tender-hearted and affectionate father,

Wm. Wordsworth.

After printing these letters the article goes on: 'The allusion to the disappointment in a letter already quoted [i.e. [A]], coupled with the recommendation to his wife and daughter to have "nothing to do with Quillinan" was probably occasioned by one of Dora's repeated refusals of his suit.'

When Professor Knight printed these letters in his *Letters of the Wordsworth Family* he rightly gave 1828 as the date of the first, and he printed the other two immediately after it, as though they were written in the same year, and only a few days later. From similar errors in their texts it is clear that Knight had not seen

[1] Error of transcription for M. W. This is a postscript added on the top of the letter by Dora's mother.
[2] John, now Vicar of Brigham, was married and had four children and a very delicate wife. Her father, Mr. Curwen, had just suffered severe financial losses.

the manuscripts of any of them, but was printing from the *Cornhill*.

Now Dora was married to Quillinan in 1841; so that her father appears to have opposed her union with him for at least thirteen years. Professor Harper, therefore, in the evidence available to him, was fully justified in his statement that 'for many years Wordsworth refused his consent to Dora's marriage'. And this view is still commonly accepted. But an examination of the manuscripts of these letters and of the Quillinan–Wordsworth correspondence shows the whole matter in a somewhat different light.

The manuscript of the letter [A], written in 1828, reads:

'Say to Mr Monkhouse, C. Wilson's behaviour shews the good sense of Dr Venables' advice, have nothing to do with Quillinan. I am sorry for his disappointment. I hope that dear Dora's looks are better,' &c.

Now it is clear from the true punctuation of this passage, that the 'have nothing to do with Q.' is not an injunction to Dora, but part of Dr. V.'s advice to Monkhouse. What C. Wilson's behaviour had been, and why Dr. Venables gave the advice does not immediately concern us; the reference is probably to some business transaction, in which Quillinan would be no safe collaborator.

The other two letters [B] and [C] are printed, both in the *Cornhill Magazine* and by Knight, with comparative accuracy, but the second of them [C] has the postmark 27 April 1839, and the other [B] will be shown to belong to a little later in the same year. Moreover, the Quillinan correspondence[1] proves that

[1] Dora tells Q. that she had burnt all his letters *before* she knew of his love for her: she kept the later ones. Q. kept all Dora's earlier letters, as well as many from Mrs. W., W. W., and Sara Hutchinson; but her letters after 1836 do not seem to have survived. But for the purpose of my article this matters little, as Q., in answering her letters, often quotes what she had said in her previous one.

though he and Dora had long loved one another, neither of them suspected the other of more than friendship till the late autumn of 1836; that the true state of affairs was not revealed to her parents till January 1838; that her father's active opposition to her engagement only lasted until the following summer; that after the summer of 1839 the only obstacle to the marriage was Quillinan's lack of means to support a wife; and that even if 'passionate jealousy' influenced the poet in his dislike of the match he had reasons which, in those days at least, many persons would have regarded as adequate.

Chief among these were the state of Dora's health and Quillinan's financial insecurity.

Dora had always been delicate, and since 1835, when she had a dangerous illness, she had never recovered her strength. She seemed, indeed, to be getting slowly weaker, she ate practically nothing, and though the doctors could not give a name to her disease, it was generally thought that she was in a decline. Clearly she needed all the watchful care and freedom from worry that a comfortable home and assured circumstances could give her. But the man who wished to marry her had not the means to support the healthiest of wives, and he was in imminent danger of losing the little that he had.

Edward Quillinan, a Roman Catholic of Irish extraction, was born at Oporto in 1791, the son of a wine merchant there. In 1808 he entered the army, and saw some service at Walcheren and in the Spanish campaign of 1814; in 1817 he married the daughter of Sir Egerton Brydges, and accompanied his regiment to Ireland and then to Scotland. In 1822 he left the army and, attracted by his admiration for Wordsworth's poetry, settled with his wife and little daughter Jemima at Rydal, where he became intimate with all the Wordsworth family. Mrs. Quillinan and Dora were soon devoted friends, and on the birth of her second child, Rotha, Dora stood godmother. In the following year Mrs. Quillinan died in tragic circumstances, her widower went abroad for a time whilst the Wordsworths looked after his children in his absence, and Dorothy Wordsworth managed for him all the business connected with his vacated house, till it could be disposed of. On his return he went with his children to live with his brother-in-law, Captain Brydges Barrett, first at Lee Priory in Kent and then in London; but his intimacy with the Wordsworths was kept up both by interchange of visits and by frequent correspondence with all members of the household. When Quillinan left the army he seems to have had a comfortable income, but though his financial affairs are shrouded in mystery it is at least clear that a few years later his means were seriously straitened and his future prospects dark. In 1826 he allowed himself to become entangled in the shady business concerns of the Brydges family, and was the participant, through careless confidence, in a fraudulent transaction by which they cleared some fifteen thousand pounds;[1] this resulted, some time later, in a lawsuit which dragged on for years and was not concluded till 1842; in 1828 he writes of 'a wicked will that has defrauded him of his just expectations', and the death of Barrett in 1834 involved him still more deeply in 'painful and difficult matters of business', so that the education of his daughters became an expense he could hardly meet. Yet though occasionally he did a little business as agent for his brother, who carried on his father's trade in Oporto, he made no serious or consistent effort to earn a living. He disliked business and evidently had little aptitude for it; moreover he was, as he said, 'cursed with elegant desires'. His delight was in the society of literary men, and in

[1] For an account of this astonishing transaction, see *The Literary Life of Sir Egerton Brydges* by Mary K. Woodworth, 1935.

dabbling in literature himself. He was a good Portuguese scholar, he wrote pleasant verses, and had, he thought, a real gift for satire, whilst his letters are proof that he had a facile pen in prose, picturesque and sometimes humorous in description. He was, too, a good talker and a pleasant companion, and there is plenty of evidence that, despite an over-sensitiveness of nature, increased, doubtless, by his precarious financial position, which made him quick to take offence and difficult to placate, he was widely popular in the society in which he moved. Not tied down to any occupation, he was often abroad. In 1831 he spent some months in Paris, superintending the education of his elder daughter, while Rotha was left in charge of the Wordsworths; in 1833 he took up his residence at Boulogne with both his daughters, saving expense by undertaking their education himself; from 1834 to 1836 he paid a long visit to his brother in Oporto. During the summer after his return he passed a month or two at Rydal, and declared his intention of settling down with his daughters at Canterbury, but in the following November he had accepted an invitation from his brother to take Jemima to Oporto for the winter, his brother paying all expenses. On his way out, in an unseaworthy ship, they had a narrow escape of drowning, and it was probably after reading his vivid account of their danger that Dora, 'by one of those acts of sudden enlightenment', as he puts it, let him into the secret of her heart, which until that moment he had never even suspected. But despite her admission Dora did not entertain the possibility of marriage to him, nor at first does he seem to have proposed it. His first love letter, dated March 1837, urges her to bring out one of her little Hutchinson cousins who had been seriously ill to join him and Jemima at Oporto: Dora replied that she could not come and would not if she could. 'It is best as it is,' she said, and she recommends him to marry someone with money. To which he replied that he would do so when she set the example, calling her 'a nun at large and her own Lady Abbess . . . but I shall be a philosopher in time'. Such throughout the year is the strain of their letters. 'My love for you', wrote Dora, 'is a spiritual Platonism, for your sake I wish you were fairly married to someone else'; but though he admits that he is 'not spiritualized enough' for her, and cannot rise to her exalted tone, he seems prepared to accept the situation.

He returned to England in October (1837), but his hopes of seeing Dora at once were frustrated, for by the time he could travel north, Dora had already left for Brinsop, whence she was going, first to London and then to winter with Miss Fenwick at Dover. But he spent a fortnight at Rydal with her parents. One evening, as he was writing to Dora, Mrs. Wordsworth entered the room and seeing Dora's last letter to him spread out on the table asked him the news. On his own confession he was 'evasive and ingenuous', and offered to read her a part of the letter, whereupon, seeing his confusion, Mrs. Wordsworth remarked that if she could only hear a part, she would rather not hear any of it. Later in the month, and also in January, the lovers met several times in London, and they travelled together down to Dover; and it was soon evident to Dora that a mere Platonic relationship would satisfy her no better than it satisfied Quillinan. Uneasy at having a secret from her parents, probably conscious, too, that their suspicions might already be aroused, Dora decided to write and break the news to her father. Quillinan warned her of his 'presentiment' that her news would not be acceptable, but the warning must have been unnecessary. Fully aware of her father's passionate love for her, she knew the terrible shock he would suffer when he learned that he had a rival in her heart. But quite apart from that wholly natural, if

unjustifiable, emotion, we can imagine how Wordsworth would regard the situation. Dora was in a state of
serious ill-health, and here was a man, who had long been
a trusted family friend, agitating her feelings in a way
that could not fail to be injurious to her, by making
love to her when he could offer her no prospect of
marriage. In his circumstances, Wordsworth must have
thought, an honourable man would have avoided her
company. On his recent visit to Rydal he had not
breathed a word of his intentions, and now he was
taking advantage of Dora's absence from her parents to
press his suit upon her when they had no opportunity
of counteracting his influence. His reply to Dora's
letter, written in the heat of the moment, must have
expressed all this in no measured terms. Quillinan
never saw it, but he judged from Dora's 'anguish' on
receiving it that it was 'cruel'. And he was probably
right in his conjecture that her father had accused him
of being 'insidious and base', and trying to 'undermine
her affection'. He wrote to Wordsworth to exculpate
himself, but did not elicit an answer; Quillinan was
deeply hurt at this, but if Wordsworth had replied, and
stated, as he would have done, how he viewed the
matter, Quillinan would probably have been hurt still
more.

Torn between a father to whom she was devoted,
who would have resented any rival, but had, she knew,
good reasons for objecting to this one, and a lover who
was now pleading with her for a definite engagement,
though he admitted in the same breath that he was
precluded by his financial straits from urging her to
influence her father in his favour, and yet that he would
marry no woman without her father's consent, poor
Dora was in a desperate position. Nor were the early
months of this year any happier for Wordsworth. For
he was obsessed with the fear that by his opposition he
had forfeited his daughter's love; and it was not for

four months that her mother could report to her any
alleviation of his despair: 'I cannot help writing to
you,' she writes at the end of April, 'though it is idle to
plague you with so many letters . . . yet we have been
more happy for the last few days than for a very long
time. Since the appearance of your being drawing [*sic*]
towards us, Father seems quite a different being.'
Fortunately for all of them they had in Miss Fenwick
a wise and faithful friend, devoted alike to Dora and to
her parents, able to see the situation from all sides, and
to enter with sympathy into the feelings of all of them.
Miss Fenwick realized that, however unfortunate Dora's
attachment might be, her health and happiness were
bound up in it, and that somehow or other the financial
obstacles must be surmounted, and that her father,
whose disapproval was causing so much pain alike to
Dora and to himself, must be brought to view the
matter with less hostility. She did what she could to
soothe and comfort Dora; and when, in the following
June, Dora returned to Rydal, Miss Fenwick accompanied her, and took up her abode in a house near by.
Then she set to work gently but insistently upon her
father, and through her mediation a compromise was
reached, 'your father reconciling himself to all objec-
tions and willing to consent when there could be any
reasonable surety of your being provided for, and there
being no hindrance to your attachment in the meantime'.[1] And then, knowing the affection that Wordsworth and Quillinan really had for one another, and
confident that if they met the old feeling would revive,
Miss Fenwick invited Quillinan to spend a few days
with her at Ambleside. Quillinan was naturally a little
nervous about accepting the invitation, but his mind
was set at ease by receiving the following letter:
My dear Mr Quillinan, you are right in supposing that you have

[1] This is Miss Fenwick's statement to Dora in April 1839, recalling
the situation that obtained in the previous year.

not forfeited my friendship, and as Dora has fully explained to you the state of my feelings I certainly do not consider it any 'intrusion' your accepting Miss Fenwick's invitation, and shall be pleased to see you at Rydal Mount.

I remain, dear Mr Quillinan, faithfully and affectionately yours,
Wm. Wordsworth.

In February (1839) Quillinan paid his visit. A week or two before coming he had written to Dora, asking her whether she would 'dare' to take the risk of marrying him without further delay, but she evaded the question, and while he was at Rydal he never broached it, except on one occasion to say to her, 'Dora, you have never answered my question'; nor did Wordsworth ever hint at the attachment, save once when he expressed to Quillinan a regret that he was a Roman Catholic. On his departure Wordsworth wrote to Southey: 'Q. left this morning on his way to Ireland. I had no private conversation with him, but through Dora he understands what my judgments and feelings are, and we all seemed at ease with one another.' His visit had at least eased the situation, even if it had not brought the marriage definitely nearer. 'I wish', he wrote to Dora on his departure, 'I could say what would be quite satisfactory to Miss Fenwick, for then you and I would be happier than we are as yet, though my visit has, I trust, removed the ill-omened gloom that darkened your house to me. How very kind Miss Fenwick has been to me! God will, I trust, favour an attachment which has excited the benevolence of a being so excellent.'

But naturally enough Quillinan was not satisfied to leave things as they were; and early in April he wrote again, urging Dora to answer his question, and making some rather vague statements about his financial position. But the time he had chosen was most unfortunate. Dora's brother Willy had long been ailing, and her parents, together with Miss Fenwick, had just taken him off to Bath to try the effect of the waters on him. Dora sent on a part of Quillinan's letter to her father, with her own comments, among them a plea that the Southey girls had been allowed to marry poor men. To this Mrs. Wordsworth answered, 'I wish you had not brought forward the Southeys, as he [i.e. her father] may readily reply that their husbands are young men and have a profession independent of their power (as proved) to increase their income, by which means they can insure their lives. Of course I shall not suggest this.' But her father found quite enough to answer in Quillinan's proposals, without touching on the Southeys. For it certainly looked as if Quillinan had been discussing the matter with Dora on his late visit, and then had again chosen the time when her parents were away to work upon her to flout their judgement and break the compact which all parties had accepted. No wonder that he wrote to Quillinan with some asperity:

Bath. 13th April

My dear Mr Quillinan,

By yesterday's post I recd. a letter from Dora, containing a long extract from one of yours to her. Upon the subject of this extract I cannot enter without premising, that calling upon her in so peremptory a manner to act on so important an occasion *during the absence of her parents*, is, to say the least of it, an ill-judged proceeding. And this I must, notwithstanding my present knowledge that the proposal you have made to her, and thro' her to me, was agitated between you when you were at Rydal; and notwithstanding anything, that appears in your letter, in justification of its being made now.

As sincerity required this declaration from me, I make no apology for it, nor do I, dear Sir, think you will require one.— I will now come to the point at once. Your letter contains these sentences, which are the only ones I shall touch upon.

'If hereafter I shall have an opportunity of making a provision for you, I will certainly do so, and I could not ask you to run the risk if I thought it possible that my death would leave you destitute of resources from my side, I have not any fear as to

that. The thing is will you *dare* to run the rough chance?'—
Before I enter upon the former sentence, I must direct your
attention to the fact, that you must have overlooked the state
of health in which Dora has long been, or you cannot have been
fully aware of it; or you could not have called upon her Parents,
thro' her, circumstanced as they are, as to age, to give their
Daughter up to '*a rough chance*'.

But from the former part of what I have copied, I must infer,
that 'tho' you can settle nothing upon her at present, you are
not without hope of being able to do so, etc. etc.'. Now it is *my
duty* to request of you, my dear Sir, to state as specifically as you
can, upon what the hopes and expectations implied or expressed
in the above Quotation from your Letter, rest. I mean in
respect of a provision in case of your death.

There is no call for my saying more till I have received your
answer upon this point, which I beg may be, on all our accounts,
as definite and explicit as possible.

Wm. is here and in a state of health that causes us much
anxiety—the Bath waters do not seem to agree with him, and
his stomach and bowels are much deranged. Miss F. owing, we
hope, solely to the severity of the weather, is not quite so well
as she was at Ambleside. We all unite in affectionate remembrances to yourself and Children, and believe me, my dear
Mr Q.,

faithfully yours,

Wm. Wordsworth.

Quillinan was deeply offended by this letter, and he
sent at once a heated and ill-judged reply which even
his best advocate Miss Fenwick strongly condemned.

'I can feel with and for you all,' she wrote to Dora, 'and for
Mr Q. too, but I do most exceedingly regret the tone of his
letter, for it has disturbed feelings which certainly were very
kindly disposed towards him, and which in time would have
been all that he could have required, and which may still be,
tho' not so soon. He ought to have taken the rebuke implied in
your father's letter more patiently; had he done so I cannot but
think that what he said of his expectations would have made
your father feel justified to himself in dispensing with an absolute security—as it is we must look for gentler movements in

his mind, and Mr Q.'s, or some circumstance that will put all into a better train again. . . . Your father will not answer Mr Q.'s letter, what more must come through you—cannot you prompt a more conciliatory letter from him? I think it is due.'

The tone of Quillinan's letter can be further conjectured by the way in which, at the same time, he wrote to Dora, losing, in his own wounded pride, all sense of what she must be suffering. He makes no attempt to answer her father's practical question, but after reviewing what seemed to him his own impeccable conduct throughout the whole affair, goes on to meet the charge of having called on her to act in her parents' absence (which, though perhaps unwittingly, he certainly had done).

'This,' he says, 'means and can mean nothing more or less than that I acted like a ————, no, that "to say the least of it, it was an ill-judged proceeding"—a cowardly attempt to work upon you and induce you to do wrong when you were deprived of the shield of their presence. No parent friendly to me, or even tolerant, could have put such a construction on any sentence I ever penned. . . . I shall never be able to discuss the subject of a union between you and me with the least chance of success for us. Then why should I submit to have my views, circumstances and pretensions discussed in syllogisms? I have been mortified enough already, and you have suffered the torments of suspense too long; you have had too painful a conflict between your love for your father and your kindness for me, and now that the hopelessness of the case is manifest I believe in my soul and conscience that you will be the less unhappy for having arrived at the conviction of its hopelessness.'

Dora had written to her mother, clearing herself and Quillinan from the charge of 'inconsideration' of her parents, and at the same time reproaching her father for making too much of financial matters; but Quillinan's letter can only have added to her despair. The good Miss Fenwick wrote to console her: 'I do not see, dear Dora, that you should view the affair as closed by anything that has as yet occurred; a little patience and gentleness will set all right.'

For despite Quillinan's letter to her father, and Dora's criticism of him which wounded him still more, Wordsworth was already relenting.

'Father's visit to London', wrote Mrs. Wordsworth on April 20, 'may forward brighter hopes and feelings than are now over-shadowing us all. But I must say that neither you nor Mr Q. do your father's feelings justice by such expressions retorted upon him as "L.S.D." and "the business of the matter". All the feelings, for your sake, that he has extinguished should not, my dearest, have been met in this spirit by either of you';

and three days later,

'We have all been calm and talk of your situation and hope of happiness as a matter decided upon—therefore, my beloved daughter, do not agitate the matter further or call upon your tender Father (for he *does* deserve that epithet if ever Man did) for more than this passive countenance, which he is, I feel, ready to give. And may his and your mother's blessing be upon you both. When you write, write as I hope you now feel, with thankfulness and hope, and in this spirit regain, if possible, your lost strength before we meet, as I trust we shall do, with hearts overflowing with love to you . . . what we owe to dear Miss Fenwick is beyond all possible conception.'

To ease the situation, Willy, a devoted son and brother, had already written both to Quillinan and Dora soothing and explanatory letters; and on the 27th, on his way to London, the poet sent his daughter the letter already printed [C]. But apparently Quillinan was still nursing his grievances: he did not write the conciliatory letter that Miss Fenwick asked for, nor, through Dora, did he make any attempt to answer the poet's practical questions, so that some ten days later Wordsworth wrote to Dora: 'I cannot but wish that you were put at rest by Mr Q. on this under all circum-stances harassing and trying affair—I wait for your report of his answer with anxiety. God bless you, my

dear daughter.' When Quillinan does reply, on May 12,
he goes far to admit the justice of her father's objec-
tions: 'I do not pretend to think that our prospects are
such as will not make many people call our marriage
madness,' and after dilating on the difficulties which
they may have to encounter in their first years of married life he says: 'My great dread as to our union has
always been lest you should find yourself removed from
a comfortable to a comfortless home . . .' (this was, of
course, just what her father feared, and was his motive
in writing the letter which Quillinan had so deeply
resented); then, on June 5, because he has not yet
received an answer to a letter written to Willy on
May 24, he breaks out 'he or some of them must have
seen my letter by this time—if they have seen my letter
and not thought proper to answer it I shall think them
all a parcel of churls and never care two twopences
more for any of them'. There seemed indeed some
doubts as to whether, now Wordsworth was in town,
Quillinan would bring himself to meet him. No wonder
that his daughter Jemima told him that 'she thought
I did not seem to be treating Mr Wordsworth with
the respectful attention due to him'. But at last he put
his injured pride in his pocket, and they met on June 8;
this was the first time, it must be remembered, that
Quillinan had ever himself stated his own case to
Wordsworth. They met again two days later and on
the 11th Quillinan wrote to Dora in a very different
mood:

'How delighted you will be, if you are really my own Dora, at
what I have to tell you! Your Father and I are right good real
friends. After that weary first interview of which I gave you a
doleful and yet half hopeful account, I never was so thoroughly
subdued in my life. That expression "too old to be trans-
planted"[1] almost killed me. . . . On Sunday Morning I went
again to Mr Marshall's by Mr W.'s appointment. I was shewn

[1] Dora was thirty-five years of age.

in to all the family at breakfast, he among them, that being his breakfast-breakfast, the one to follow at Kenyon's was to be his talking breakfast. Presently he went with me into the library and there read me that most kind letter which he had written to you [i.e. the letter already quoted as [B]]. From that moment all was right. I dismounted from my high horse, never more to get on its back, by my fault at least, to him. Willy kindly gave me his seat in the Cabriolet and walked to Kenyon's, that I might ride with his father to Harley Street. In the Cab. he spoke to me with all the affection of a friend and a father, and if he holds to that, it must be my delight as well as my duty to shew that that *is the right course.*'

But poor Dora's troubles were not yet over. For some time her father found it difficult to feel consistently towards his future son-in-law as a friend and a father; and it is probably of this time, as well as the previous summer, of which Taylor, whose informant was Miss Fenwick, speaks in the passage quoted at the beginning of this paper. In September Quillinan wrote to Dora that he had not the same pleasure in going to Rydal as in the past, and complained that her father was still trying to exert his influence against him. But that is the last suggestion in his letters that he had anything to complain of in the poet's attitude either to him or to the marriage, and his natural sensitiveness was such that if he had had any grievance to air we can be sure that he would have felt no scruple in airing it. In December it is not of her father but of his poverty that he complains. He admits that his affairs do not justify their marriage. 'Oh Dora, so I have been to Rydal and come away again as usual leaving you behind me, without any definite time or plan for claiming you. I will not, however, be dolorous. Something *must* turn up in our favour, the cards have been against us so long.' A friend, he tells her, has just asked him why he does not marry. 'Because we are too poor.' 'Nonsense,' she says, 'He without whose notice not a sparrow falls will not allow true love to starve.' 'It is true she does not know how very poor I am, nor any of the particulars of my circumstances (how I hate the word), but she knows that I have been very unlucky and much bothered.' Apparently he seems at last to have realized himself that if you marry an invalid wife it is as well to have the means to support her.

And throughout the next year, though the marriage is still delayed, there is no sign of friction. In the early months when Dora was in London, enjoying the society of Quillinan and her other friends, the correspondence that passed between her father and lover was cordial; and in the summer, which he spent at Rydal, Quillinan wrote to his daughter Rotha in a tone which suggests that his old affection for the poet had returned. And Quillinan did not make it easier for Wordsworth. For not content with having secured an obviously reluctant consent to the marriage he was now insisting that Wordsworth should come to the wedding and give his daughter away. Crabb Robinson justly wrote that he thought this 'was too much to ask'. But here again Wordsworth gave way, and in the following May the marriage took place. Whether Quillinan's income had improved we do not know, but it seems certain that Wordsworth gave his daughter some financial help, though some years passed before he made her a definite allowance. Indeed, at this time he could hardly have done so; he was past seventy and was on the point of resigning in favour of his son William the post from which he derived £400 a year, more than half his income; and he was not placed on the civil list till eighteen months later. Knowing the strength of his passions, there were those who feared that when it came to the point some of his old resentment at the match might burst into a flame. But they were mistaken. On May 8 Miss Fenwick wrote, 'Our marriage stands for the 11th, and I do sincerely trust nothing will interfere with its taking place on that day, for all parties concerned are prepared for it. Mr. Wordsworth behaves beautifully.'

And so he behaved after the marriage. In the following year when the Brydges lawsuit came to a head, and Quillinan was in danger of losing not merely his income but his honour, Wordsworth wrote him this generous letter:

My dear Quillinan,

Your letter to Miss Fenwick moved me much on many accounts. But my motive for writing this short letter is merely to assure you of our sympathy in your vexations and distresses, and still more, very much more, to assure you that you need have no anxiety respecting judgment which we are likely to form of your character on these sad proceedings. We have all an entire confidence in your integrity from the first to the last, in your connection with the Brydges family, and the Barrett property, and furthermore are but too well aware of the generous sacrifices which you have made for them who have proved to be so unworthy of them. The confidence you reposed in them, however chargeable it may be with want of discretion, affords itself a strong presumption of your being incapable of joining in any dishonorable transaction. As I have confidence that you will regulate your mind as becomes you, I have nothing to add but the expression of a wish that the business may be speedily brought to a close, with as little injustice as is possible under the untoward circumstances which the wicked arts of the adverse party have produced.

Believe me, my dear Q., affectionately yours

Wm. Wordsworth.

March 1st 1842

The result of the trial can be learned from Crabb Robinson's diary for April 1842. 'I was glad to read in *The Times* a declaration from the Vice-Chancellor that he believed Mr Q. was free from all intention to commit any fraud, but he is made liable with some 4 or 5 others to make up the difference between £22,000 and £7,000, besides costs, which will be a sad dead weight lying on him and prevent his doing anything for his wife.'

This news can only have strengthened Wordsworth in his conviction that his opposition to the match had been justified; nor indeed was he ever reconciled to it. To Dora, as ever, he remained passionately devoted, and with her husband he kept upon the best of terms, but there can be little doubt that he did not hide his feelings about it from his wife; whilst to Miss Fenwick, the dearest friend of his old age, who had been the stoutest advocate of the marriage, he did not scruple to speak his mind. He liked Quillinan as a man, and was ready to allow him many good qualities; but, like many parents who have lost their daughters to better sons-in-law than his, he did not think him good enough for Dora, quite apart from all financial considerations; and his letters to Miss Fenwick contain several pregnant reflections on the incomprehensibility of woman's choice of a mate. Moreover he thought Quillinan selfish and inconsiderate. After a visit to his daughter in 1844 he wrote:

'The knowledge that my presence was useful to Dora recompensed me in no small degree for unpleasantness of a domestic kind which you are not ignorant of. The worst of it is that Mr Q. seems incapable of regulating his own temper according to the demands which his wife's indisposition too frequently makes upon it, and it is not to be doubted that his way of spending his time is little suited to make the day pass pleasantly for others. He never scarcely *converses* with his wife and daughters; his papers, his books, or a newspaper, engross all his time. This is surely deplorable; and yet, poor Creature, she is very fond of him, and this I suppose must happen mostly if married pairs do not positively dislike each other—indifference can scarcely exist under that connection except in minds altogether barren or trivial.'

But what he chiefly resented was Quillinan's reluctance to make any effort to earn a living for himself and his wife, and his apparent complacency in living to a great extent on the bounty of others. This was the poet's reason for declining to grant Dora a regular allowance when Miss Fenwick first urged it upon him. 'I will not bind myself,' he said, 'circumstanced as Dora is, to make her any fixed allowance. I am convinced it would be wrong to do so, as it would only provoke in certain quarters an effect which I should exceedingly deprecate'; and again a little later, after speaking of Quillinan's general kindness and amiability, he goes on:

'Neither this, however, nor anything else, reconciles me to his course of life. You say he could not procure employment—I say he does not try—the fact is he cannot bring himself to stoop in the direction he ought to stoop in. His pride looks and works the wrong way, and I am hopeless of a cure—but I am resolved not to minister to it, because it ought not to exist, circumstanced as he is. His inaction mortifies me the more because his talents are greatly superior to those of most men who earn a handsome livelihood by literature.'

But again, by gentle but insistent pressure, Miss Fenwick won her point, and the allowance was granted. Quillinan has been praised for asking, after Dora's death, that the payment should be discontinued; but how could he possibly have accepted it? And if in this his nice sense of honour stood him in good stead, that morbid sensitiveness which was bound up with it could still lead him to crass misconstruction of the motives and feelings of others. For when the poet, in his uncontrollable grief at Dora's death, could not bring himself to cross the bridge that led to her house, Quillinan interpreted it as a deliberate insult aimed at himself.

This last incident serves to emphasize what must be obvious to all who have followed the story, that Dora's father and her lover lived emotionally upon different planes, so that it was difficult for either of them to do full justice to the other. Quillinan, entirely sincere and genuine in his affections, was yet a man of the normal emotional calibre: Wordsworth was a man of intensely passionate feeling. 'Few know', remarked

Rogers, a shrewd man of the world, not given to over-statement, '*how* Wordsworth loves his friends'; and his passions were nowhere stronger than where his children were concerned. Aubrey de Vere relates how, forty years after the death of Catharine and Thomas, the poet 'described the details of their illnesses with an exactness and intensity of troubled excitement such as might have been expected if the bereavement had taken place but a few weeks before'; and no one can read his letters without noting that his anxiety about the health of those dear to him amounted to an obsession. Dora was the darling of his old age; when her marriage was first mooted she was dangerously ill, and, firmly con-vinced of the risk involved in her union to a man who could ill afford to support her, it was inevitable that he should be difficult to convince that an even greater risk might be involved in opposing a match on which her heart was set. To what extent this conviction was strengthened by a selfish desire to keep Dora for him-self, no one can determine, for all human motives are mixed; but if at times he thought more of himself than Dora, Quillinan's letters during the crisis prove that his wounded vanity, a less excusable motive, led him to do the same.

And further, Wordsworth differed from Quillinan in his whole attitude to the practical concerns of life. That passion and imagination which are essential constituents in a great poet were in him combined with a thoroughly realistic turn of mind. To this combination his poetry owes its distinctive character; to this it owed also that weakness which Coleridge aptly described as 'matter-of-factness': in the issues of daily life it was manifested in a resolute insistence on facing the facts, and seeing things as they are. He had indeed all the caution and the hard-headedness of the typical north-countryman. He had known poverty in his youth and early manhood, and later the dilatory slackness of his brother Richard in money matters had impressed on him still further the importance of straight dealing and of meeting a situation instead of shirking it. Dora and her lover might reproach him for thinking too much of 'L.S.D.', and the unworldly Miss Fenwick might abet their romantic illusions, but he knew from experience, that if we live in this world and not in some far-off Utopia, to ignore the part played by 'L.S.D.' in our happiness is simply a dangerous folly; and he could not bring himself to countenance it. But to such mundane considerations Quillinan showed a lofty indifference. The financial difficulties in which his careless generosity had involved him had become for him the excuse for making no effort to earn his own living. His Micawber-like words to Dora, 'something *must* turn up in our favour' sum up his attitude to life. He never faced the situation or made any effort to retrieve it; but, sensitive as he was of his honour, he was yet content to live for the most part upon the hospitality of others, with no real sense of responsibility. How exasperating this must have been to Wordsworth can easily be imagined. That two men so radically different in outlook should have been good friends where no practical issues were at stake between them is nothing to wonder at: that they should have remained so as father and son-in-law is, in reality, a striking tribute to both of them, and, perhaps still more, to the woman whom they both loved.

III

COLERIDGE'S *DEJECTION: AN ODE*[1]

STUDENTS of Coleridge have sometimes been puzzled by the entry in Dorothy Wordsworth's *Journal* under the date 21 April 1802:

'William and I sauntered in the garden. Coleridge came to us, and repeated the verses he wrote to Sara. I was affected with them, and in miserable spirits. The sunshine, the green fields and the fair sky made me sadder; even the little happy sporting lambs seemed but sorrowful to me. . . . I went to bed after dinner, could not sleep. . . .'

What were these verses of Coleridge's that so deeply affected his friends? When Professor Knight edited the *Journal* he appended to the passage this note: 'Can these verses have been the first draft of *Dejection: an Ode*, in its earliest and afterwards abandoned form? It is said to have been written on 2nd April 1802.'[2] Similarly Mr. T. M. Raysor remarks in his essay entitled 'Coleridge and Asra',[3] 'The supposed first draft (to Wordsworth) may in reality be a second draft, developing the poem and adapting it to a different purpose in order to conceal its original application'.

The version of the ode now published, as it was written on 4 April 1802, and sent to Sara Hutchinson, proves this conjecture to be correct.

The *textus receptus* of the poem is that which Coleridge printed in his *Sybilline Leaves* of 1817, but before this he had published it in the *Morning Post* of

---

[1] From *Essays and Studies by Members of the English Association*, vol. xxii, 1937.

[2] Even in making this happy conjecture Knight is inaccurate. The ode was not 'said to be written on 2nd' April, it is definitely stated by Coleridge to have been written on April 4.

[3] In *Studies in Philology*, July 1929. A valuable essay, which sets forth with sympathy and understanding the course of Coleridge's love for Sara Hutchinson.

7 October 1802. The two texts differ in several minor details:[1] the main variations between them are that (1) 'Edmund', a transparent sobriquet for Wordsworth, is found in the *Morning Post* for the vaguer 'Lady' of the *T.R.*; (2) lines 87–93 (*T.R.*)

> For not to think of what I needs must feel
> But to be still and patient, all I can;
> And haply by abstruse research to steal
> From my own nature all the natural man—
> This was my sole resource, my only plan:
> Till that which suits a part infects the whole,
> And now is almost grown the habit of my soul,

are omitted from the *M.P.*; (3) in the concluding lines that Joy which in the *T.R.* the poet invokes for the 'lady' is in the *M.P.* represented as already the possession of his poet friend:

> With light heart may he rise,
> Gay fancy, cheerful eyes,
> And sing his lofty song, and teach me to rejoice!
> O Edmund, friend of my devoutest choice,
> O rais'd from anxious dread and busy care,
> By the immenseness of the good and fair,
> Which thou see'st everywhere,
> Joy lifts thy spirit, joy attunes thy voice,
> To thee do all things live from pole to pole,
> Their life the eddying of thy living soul!
> O simple Spirit, guided from above,
> O lofty Poet, full of life and love,
> Brother and Friend of my devoutest choice,
> Thus may'st thou ever, evermore rejoice!

Other manuscript versions of the poem, or part of it, are also extant. Two copies were transcribed for Sir George Beaumont, one of which, at least, must belong to the period between the composition of the poem and

[1] An exhaustive collation of all hitherto known texts of the poem will be found in the Clarendon Press edition of Coleridge's *Complete Poetical Works*, ed. by E. H. Coleridge. In this article the *textus eceptus* is referred to as *T.R.*

its appearance in the *M.P.*;[1] in this copy 'William' is
substituted for the 'Edmund' of the *M.P.* Another is
found in a letter to William Sotheby dated 19 July 1802,
in which, after speaking of how 'sickness and some other
and worse afflictions first forced me into downright
metaphysics', he goes on, 'For I believe that by nature
I have more of the poet in me. In a poem written
during that dejection, to Wordsworth, and the greater
part of a private nature, I thus expressed the thought
in language more forcible than harmonious'; and then,
after quoting stanza vi ('There was a time, &c. . . . soul')
(*T.R.* ll. 76–93), he continues, 'Thank heaven! my
better mind has returned to me, and I trust I shall go
on rejoicing. As I have nothing better to fill the space
of this sheet with, I will transcribe the introduction of
that poem to you, that being of a sufficiently general
nature to be interesting to you.' Much of the poem
follows in a version similar to that published in the
M.P., but with 'Wordsworth' for 'Edmund', and a few
other variants.

Ten days later Coleridge wrote to Southey in something of the same strain:

'As to myself, all my poetic genius (if ever I really possessed any
genius, and it was not rather a more general aptitude of talent
and quickness in imitation) is gone, and I have been fool enough
to suffer deeply in my mind, regretting the loss, which I
attribute to my long and exceedingly severe metaphysical in-
vestigations, and these partly to ill-health, and partly to private
afflictions which rendered any subjects immediately connected
with feeling a source of pain and disquiet to me.'

He then quotes *T.R.*, ll. 76–86, after which he says,

'here follow a dozen lines that would give you no pleasure,[2] and
then what follows:—"For not to think," &c. [*T.R.* ll. 87–93].

[1] Knight, confusing the date of composition with that of transcription, says that 'it was transcribed for Sir G. B. on the 4th of April'.
This is impossible.

[2] Naturally, for they are the lines which bewail his 'coarse domestic
life', and his disagreement with Mrs. Coleridge, Southey's sister-in-law.

Having written these lines, I rejoice for you as well as for myself, that I am able to inform you, that now for a long time there has been more love and concord in my house than I have known for years before.'

It is hardly necessary to state that the love and concord which reigned at Greta Hall during July and August 1802 was only a brief suspension of hostilities: hence *Dejection: an Ode* is the record, not of a passing mood now happily surmounted, but rather of a brilliant poetic genius doomed to premature frustration. A review of Coleridge's relations with the two Saras up to the date of its composition may serve to elucidate the poem, and in particular those lines 'of a private nature', which are now printed for the first time.

Coleridge had engaged himself to Sarah Fricker in August 1794 in the interests of pantisocracy, and within a month of his rejection by Mary Evans, whom for the previous four years he had loved 'almost to madness'. If he had hoped that this new attachment would efface the old one he was mistaken. 'Every day', he wrote a few months later, 'her memory sinks deeper into my breast', whilst of Sarah he speaks as 'her whom I do not love, but whom by every tie of reason and honour I ought to love. I am resolved, but wretched.' He was married on 4 October 1795, and in the novelty of the situation he seems for a time to have been really happy. Sarah has now become 'the woman whom I love best of all created beings', and the birth of Hartley in the next year, and of Berkeley in May 1798, by giving them a common interest, served to keep them united. The incursion of the Wordsworths into their family circle seems, in the Nether Stowey days, to have caused no unpleasantness, but rather, by the diversion it caused for Coleridge, to have postponed the day when he would realize his wife's limitations; and in his letters to her from Germany there is no trace of any waning of his affection. Only on his return, in July 1799, did he

realize the emptiness of his home when the Wordsworths were beyond his reach; and when, on October
26, he joined them at Sockburn, met Mary and Sara
Hutchinson for the first time, and was welcomed into
a society of wellnigh perfect intellectual and emotional
harmony, the contrast with his own home life must
have struck him all the more deeply. On the next day
he left with Wordsworth to pay his first visit to the
Lake country, but returning to Sockburn alone, he
stayed there nearly a week. On November 24 he recorded in his private note-book,[1] 'Stood up round the
fire, et Sarae manum a tergo longum in tempus pren-
satam, ad tunc temporis, tunc primum amor levi spiculo
venenato eheu et insanabili'. The love for Sara Hutchinson then awakened proved to be the deepest and most
permanent passion of his life; his ballad *Love*, sent to the
Morning Post on December 21, is his first poetic tribute
to it.

Thus when Coleridge brought his family to reside
at Keswick in the following summer the Wordsworths
were not the only attraction that lured him to the
north; and for the next few years he saw much of Sara
Hutchinson. Before her visit to Grasmere in November–December 1800 she and the Wordsworths spent
some days at Greta Hall, and while she was at Dove
Cottage Coleridge was often there; during the next
spring she was again the guest of both the Coleridges
and the Wordsworths, and in the following August,
under the pretext of sea-bathing, Coleridge spent a
week with the Hutchinsons at Gallow Hill, near Scar-
borough.

How far Mrs. Coleridge realized the extent of her
husband's devotion to Sara can only be conjectured,
but it is clear that she resented his absorption in the

---

[1] For permission to inspect these note-books I am indebted to the
courtesy of the Rev. Gerald Coleridge. Mr. Raysor's article (q.v.) is
chiefly based on a careful examination of them.

society of the whole Wordsworth circle, which she felt
all the more because, removed from all her own friends
at Nether Stowey and Bristol, she was the more de-
pendent upon his company. What wonder, then, that
he had to complain of the 'freezing looks' with which
she greeted his visitors, and Dorothy to admit that they
were 'never very comfortable at Greta Hall after two
or three days', after which time their company 'ceased
to do Coleridge any good'? Moreover, he had hardly
settled at Keswick before his health gave way. For nine
months, he wrote in July 1801, he had had barely a
fortnight's continued health, suffering from giddy head,
sick stomach, and swollen knees; to ease his rheumatic
pains he had recourse to opium, and now for the first
time became its slave. And as he was seldom long
at home when he was well enough to leave it, Mrs.
Coleridge had for the most part a sick man upon her
hands, irritable, depressed, often under the influence
of narcotics. It would have been trying for her if she
had been a trained nurse and a perfect wife. The
Wordsworths, despite their love for Coleridge, could
sympathize with her difficulties. 'She is indeed a bad
nurse for Coleridge', wrote Dorothy, 'but she has
several great merits. She is much, very much to be
pitied, for when one party is ill-matched the other
necessarily must be so too. She would have made a very
good wife for many another man, but for Coleridge!!
Her radical fault is want of sensibility, and what can
such a woman be to Coleridge?'

The situation grew daily more desperate. In October
1801 Coleridge wrote to Southey, his wife's brother-in-
law, as if to prepare him for an imminent crisis. He has,
he says, completely thought through the subject of
marriage, and is deeply convinced of its indissoluble-
ness, but though he goes on hoping that all will end
happily he is convinced that if this mutual unsuitable-
ness continues and strengthens he and Mrs. Coleridge

had better separate. His grief is all the greater in that
it will mean a separation from his children. 'If my wife
loved me, and I my wife, half as well as we both love
our children, I should be the happiest man alive, but
this is not—will not be.'

In November he left for London, visiting Sara
Hutchinson on his way, and for the next few months
wrote letter after letter to her and to the Wordsworths,
pouring out his woes. It is difficult for us to share
their sympathy with him, when we read in Dorothy's
Journals how relentlessly he preyed upon their love,
often causing them sleepless nights, and affecting
their health and spirits by his reiterated complaints.
Dorothy's entry for 29 January 1802 is typical: 'A
heart-rending letter from C. We were sad as we could
be. Wm wrote to him. We talked of Wm's going to
London.' Coleridge was fully conscious of the sorrow
that he brought upon them, and bitterly reproached
himself for it, but he had not the self-control to spare
them, and he always chose to write to them at those
moments when he was in his most abject mood. For
he was not so consistently miserable as he led them to
suppose. Indeed, as the time approached for his return
to Keswick he could write to his wife of the 'tranquil
state of his mind' and 'the cheerfulness inspired by the
thought of speedily returning to you in love and peace.
I drive away every thought but those of hope and of the
tenderest yearnings after you.'

But if he felt these tender yearnings he did not
pursue a course most likely to perpetuate them; for
on his way home he passed some days at Gallow Hill.
Reaching home in the middle of March, with the
memory of Mary and Sara's loving ministrations[1] still

---

[1] It was upon this visit to Gallow Hill that the incident described in
ll. 99–110 of the *Ode* must have taken place. For when C. was at Gallow
Hill in the previous November Mary was at Grasmere. His other visit
was in August, and the passage suggests winter rather than summer.

fresh in his mind, he was not, perhaps, in the best frame of mind to appreciate a wife whose 'radical fault was a want of sensibility'.

'After my return to Keswick', he wrote later, 'I was, if possible, more miserable than before. Scarce a day passed without such a scene of discord between me and Mrs. C. as quite incapacitated me from any worthy exertion of my faculties, by degrading me in my own estimation. I found my temper impaired and daily more so; the good and pleasurable thoughts which had been the support of my moral character departed from my solitude. I determined to go abroad, but alas! the less I loved my wife the more dear and necessary did my children seem to me. I found no comfort except in the driest speculation.'[1]

Within a few days he was over at Grasmere. On March 19 Dorothy's *Journal* has the significant entry: 'Coleridge came in. His eyes were a little swollen with the wind. I was much affected by the sight of him. He seemed half stupified. William came in soon after. Coleridge went to bed late, and William and I sate up till four o'clock.' Doubtless their conversation was chiefly of Coleridge and his troubles. He stayed with them two days, and a week later they followed him to Keswick. Dorothy's report of their visit is brief and non-committal, though the entry under April 4, 'we sate pleasantly enough after supper', suggests, perhaps, that at other times things had not gone too smoothly. It was upon that night that Coleridge wrote, or more probably completed, *Dejection: an Ode*.

It is obvious that Coleridge could never have published that part of the poem to which he refers as 'of a private nature', even if it had been poetically equal to the rest; nor could he have printed any of it as an address to Sara Hutchinson. For though he made no secret of his alienation from his wife, his attachment to Sara was unknown outside the Wordsworth circle. Yet, when he told Sotheby that the poem was addressed to Words-

[1] To Thomas Wedgwood, 20 October 1802.

worth, and implied it by the form of its publication in
the *Morning Post*, though he is concealing some of the
facts, he can hardly be held guilty of misrepresentation.
For even as it was first written the poem is a psychological analysis, as acute as it is tragic, of his own mental
and emotional state viewed throughout in conscious
and deliberate contrast with that of his poet friend.
The lines bewailing his own domestic woes are conceived with the perfect affection and harmony of Dove
Cottage vividly present in his mind, even the lines
more definitely addressed to Sara are written with a
sense—and herein lies much of their pathos—that
though she returned his love, she yet belonged intrin-
sically, not to him, but to that happy company of
friends, Mary and Dorothy and William, from which,
despite their sympathy with him, his own misery
seemed more and more to shut him out. This contrast
in their fortunes was already, he felt, evident in their
respective poetic achievements. For he believed with
no less conviction than Wordsworth that 'the deep
power of joy' was alike the inspiration and the true
basis of all sane imaginative art. Wordsworth, despite
the troubles and anxieties of his life, was essentially
'a happy man and therefore bold to look on painful
things': of Coleridge he remarked years later,[1] 'It was
poor dear Coleridge's constant infelicity that prevented
him from being the poet that Nature had given him
the power to be. He had always too much personal
and domestic discontent to paint the sorrows of mankind. He could not afford to suffer with those whom
he saw suffer.' This is but a restatement of the view
maintained by Coleridge himself in many of his letters
no less than in the *Ode*. He was broken by 'afflictions
which rendered any subjects immediately connected
with feeling a source of pain and disquiet to me', and

[1] Barron Field's *Memoirs of the Life and Poetry of William Wordsworth* (B.M. MS.).

'when a man is unhappy he writes damned bad poetry'; or, probably, if he is also a good critic, he will not write at all. Hence, he feels, while his friend will go on from strength to strength, he is himself doomed to poetic sterility.

That this contrast between Wordsworth and himself was the root idea of *Dejection* becomes doubly clear when we relate the facts already given of Coleridge's life with those of Wordsworth during the same period. The birth of his love for Sara was almost coincident with his discovery of Wordsworth's love for Mary, and while he knew that his love could never be fully satisfied, he saw his friend approaching nearer and nearer to his goal. When Wordsworth, in the company of his loved sister, paid his visit to Keswick in March–April 1802, he was on his way to see Mary, with a view to arranging that marriage which was to set the seal upon his happiness. A few days before he left Grasmere he had composed his triumphant lyric *The Rainbow* and the first stanzas of his great *Ode*; and though those stanzas only state the problem, and the *Ode* was not to be completed till more than a year later, he must have recited to Coleridge what he had already written, and spoken to him of that mood of meditative ecstasy in which his poem was to close. For lines 136 and 295 of *Dejection*—'I too will crown me with a Coronal', and 'They are not to me now the Things, which once they were'—are deliberate reminiscences, which Wordsworth could not fail to notice, of line 40 and line 9 of his own *Ode*. As we have seen, Coleridge wrote *Dejection* while Wordsworth was still under his roof; and soon after Wordsworth had returned to Grasmere, his joyful mission to Mary accomplished, Coleridge came over and repeated to him and Dorothy 'the verses he wrote to Sara'. A revised version of them appeared in the *Morning Post* of October 7, Wordsworth's wedding-day.

A LETTER TO ——

April 4, 1802.   Sunday Evening.

Well! if the Bard was weatherwise, who made
The grand old Ballad of Sir Patrick Spence,
This Night, so tranquil now, will not go hence
Unrous'd by winds, that ply a busier trade
Than that, which moulds yon clouds in lazy flakes,   5
Or the dull sobbing Draft, that drones and rakes
Upon the Strings of this Eolian Lute,
Which better far were mute.
For, lo! the New Moon, winter-bright!
And overspread with phantom Light   10
(With swimming phantom Light o'erspread
But rimm'd and circled with a silver Thread)
I see the Old Moon in her Lap, foretelling
The coming-on of Rain and squally Blast—
O! Sara! that the Gust ev'n now were swelling,   15
And the slant Night-shower driving loud and fast!

A Grief without a pang, void, dark and drear,
A stifling, drowsy, unimpassion'd Grief
That finds no natural outlet, no Relief
In word, or sigh, or tear—   20
This, Sara! well thou know'st,
Is that sore Evil, which I dread the most,
And oft'nest suffer! In this heartless Mood,
To other thoughts by yonder Throstle woo'd,
That pipes within the Larch tree, not unseen,   25
(The Larch, which pushes out in tassels green
It's bundled Leafits) woo'd to mild Delights
By all the tender Sounds and gentle Sights
Of this sweet Primrose-month—and *vainly* woo'd
O dearest Sara! in this heartless Mood   30
All this long Eve, so balmy and serene,
Have I been gazing on the western Sky
And its peculiar Tint of Yellow Green—
And still I gaze—and with how blank an eye!
And those thin Clouds above, in flakes and bars,   35
That give away their Motion to the Stars;

Those Stars, that glide behind them, or between,
Now sparkling, now bedimm'd, but always seen;
Yon crescent Moon, as fix'd as if it grew
In it's own cloudless, starless Lake of Blue—   40
A boat becalm'd! dear William's Sky Canoe!
—I see them all, so excellently fair!
I see, not feel, how beautiful they are.

My genial Spirits fail—
And what can these avail   45
To lift the smoth'ring Weight from off my Breast?
It were a vain Endeavor,
Tho' I should gaze for ever
On that Green Light which lingers in the West!
I may not hope from outward Forms to win   50
The Passion and the Life, whose Fountains are within!

These lifeless Shapes, around, below, Above,
    O what can they impart?
When even the gentle Thought, that thou, my Love!
Art gazing, now, like me,   55
And see'st the Heaven, I see—
Sweet Thought it is—yet feebly stirs my Heart!

Feebly! O feebly!—Yet
(I well remember it)
In my first Dawn of Youth that Fancy stole   60
With many secret Yearnings on my Soul.
At eve, sky-gazing in 'ecstatic fit'
(Alas! for cloister'd in a city School
The Sky was all, I knew, of Beautiful)
At the barr'd window often did I sit,   65
And oft upon the leaded School-roof lay,
And to myself would say—

41. *v.* Prologue to *Peter Bell.*
63–6. Cf. *Frost at Midnight*, 51–3:
          For I was reared
     In the great city, pent 'mid cloisters dim
     And saw naught lovely but the sky and stars.

There does not live the Man so stripp'd of good affections
As not to love to see a Maiden's quiet Eyes
Uprais'd, and linking on sweet Dreams by dim Connections 70
To Moon, or Evening Star, or glorious western Skies—
While yet a Boy, this Thought would so pursue me,
That often it became a kind of Vision to me!

Sweet Thought! and dear of old
To Hearts of finer Mould!   75
Ten thousand times by Friends and Lovers blest!
I spake with rash Despair,
And ere I was aware,
The Weight was somewhat lifted from my Breast!
O Sara! in the weather-fended Wood,   80
Thy lov'd haunt! where the Stock-doves coo at Noon
I guess, that thou hast stood
And watch'd yon Crescent, and it's ghost-like Moon.
And yet, far rather in my present Mood
I would, that thou'dst been sitting all this while   85
Upon the sod-built Seat of Camomile—
And tho' thy Robin may have ceas'd to sing,
Yet needs for *my* sake must thou love to hear
The Bee-hive murmuring near,
That ever-busy and most quiet Thing   90
Which I have heard at Midnight murmuring.

I feel my spirit moved.
And wheresoe'er thou be,
O Sister! O Beloved!
Those dear mild Eyes, that see   95
Even now the Heaven, *I* see—
There is a Prayer in them! It is for *me*—
And I, dear Sara, *I* am blessing *thee*!

It was as calm as this, that happy night
When Mary, thou, and I together were,   100

89–91. Cf. *A Day-dream*, l. 35: Like the still hive at quiet mid-night humming.

99–110. This incident is made the theme of a separate poem, *A Day-dream*, first published in the *Bijou*, 1828.

The low decaying Fire our only Light,
And listen'd to the Stillness of the Air!
O that affectionate and blameless Maid,
Dear Mary! on her Lap my head she lay'd—
Her Hand was on my Brow,   105
Even as my own is now;
And on my Cheek I felt the eye-lash play.
Such joy I had, that I may truly say,
My Spirit was awe-stricken with the Excess
And trance-like Depth of it's brief Happiness.   110

Ah fair Remembrances, that so revive
The Heart, and fill it with a living Power,
Where were they, Sara?—or did I not strive
To win them to me?—on the fretting Hour
Then when I wrote thee that complaining Scroll,   115
Which even to bodily Sickness bruis'd thy Soul!
And yet thou blam'st thyself alone! And yet
Forbidd'st me all Regret!

And must I not regret, that I distress'd
Thee, best belov'd, who lovest me the best?   120
My better mind had fled, I know not whither,
For O! was this an absent Friend's Employ
To send from far both Pain and Sorrow thither
Where still his Blessings should have call'd down Joy!
I read thy guileless Letter o'er again—   125
I hear thee of thy blameless Self complain—
And only this I learn—and this, alas! I know—
That thou art weak and pale with Sickness, Grief, and Pain—
And *I,—I* made thee so!

O for my own sake I regret perforce   130
Whatever turns thee, Sara! from the course
Of calm Well-being and a Heart at rest!
When thou, and with thee those, whom thou lov'st best,
Shall dwell together in one happy Home,
One House, the dear *abiding* Home of All,   135
I too will crown me with a Coronal—
Nor shall this Heart in idle Wishes roam
     Morbidly soft!

     136. Cf. Wordsworth's *Ode*, l. 40: My heart hath its coronal.

No! let me trust, that I shall wear away
In no inglorious Toils the manly Day,   140
And only now and then, and not too oft,
Some dear and memorable Eve will bless
Dreaming of all your Loves and Quietness.
Be happy, and I need thee not in sight.
Peace in thy Heart, and Quiet in thy Dwelling,   145
Health in thy Limbs, and in thine eyes the Light
Of Love and Hope and honorable Feeling—
Where e'er I am, I shall be well content!
Not near thee, haply shall be more content!
To all things I prefer the Permanent.   150
And better seems it, for a Heart, like mine,
Always to *know*, than sometimes to behold,
    Their Happiness and thine—
For Change doth trouble me with pangs untold!
To see thee, hear thee, feel thee—then to part   155
    Oh! it weighs down the heart!
To *visit* those, I love, as I love thee,
Mary, and William, and dear Dorothy,
It is but a temptation to repine—
The transientness is Poison in the Wine,   160
Eats out the pith of Joy, makes all Joy hollow,
All Pleasure a dim Dream of Pain to follow!
My own peculiar Lot, my house-hold Life
It is, and will remain, Indifference or Strife.
While *Ye* are *well* and *happy*, 'twould but wrong you 165
If I should fondly yearn to be among you—
Wherefore, O wherefore! should I wish to be
A wither'd branch upon a blossoming Tree?

But (let me say it! for I vainly strive
To beat away the Thought), but if thou pin'd   170
Whate'er the Cause, in body or in mind,
I were the miserablest Man alive
To know it and be absent! Thy Delights
Far off, or near, alike I may partake—
But O! to mourn for thee, and to forsake   175
All power, all hope, of giving comfort to thee—
To know that thou art weak and worn with pain,
And not to hear thee, Sara! not to view thee—

Not sit beside thy Bed,
Not press thy aching Head,   180
Not bring thee Health again—
At least to hope, to try—
By this Voice, which thou lov'st, and by this earnest Eye—
Nay, wherefore did I let it haunt my Mind
The dark distressful Dream!   185
I turn from it, and listen to the Wind
Which long has rav'd unnotic'd! What a Scream
Of agony, by Torture lengthen'd out
That Lute sent forth! O thou wild Storm without!
Jagg'd Rock, or mountain Pond, or blasted Tree,   190
Or Pine-Grove, whither Woodman never clomb,
Or lonely House, long held the Witches' Home,
Methinks were fitter Instruments for Thee,
Mad Lutanist! that in this month of Showers,
Of dark brown Gardens and of peeping Flowers,   195
Mak'st Devil's Yule with worse than wintry Song
The Blossoms, Buds, and timorous Leaves among!
Thou Actor, perfect in all tragic Sounds!
Thou mighty Poet, even to frenzy bold!
What tell'st thou now about?   200
'Tis of the Rushing of an Host in Rout
And many groans for men with smarting Wounds—
At once they groan with smart, and shudder with the cold!
'Tis hush'd! there is a Trance of deepest Silence,
Again! but all that Sound, as of a rushing Crowd,   205
And Groans and tremulous Shudderings, all are over.
And it has other Sounds, and all less deep, less loud!
A Tale of less Affright,
And temper'd with Delight,
As William's self had made the tender Lay—   210
'Tis of a little Child
Upon a heathy Wild,
Not far from home, but it has lost it's way—
And now moans low in utter grief and fear—
And now screams loud, and hopes to make it's Mother hear!

210–15. An allusion to Wordsworth's *Lucy Gray.* Cf. also Letter to
Poole, 1 February 1801 'This night-wind that pipes its thin, doleful,
climbing, sinking notes, like a child that has lost its way and is crying

'Tis Midnight! and small Thoughts have I of Sleep.   216
Full seldom may my Friend such Vigils keep—
O breathe She softly in her gentle Sleep!
Cover her, gentle Sleep! with wings of Healing.
And be this Tempest but a Mountain Birth!   220
May all the Stars hang bright above her Dwelling,
Silent, as though they *watch'd* the sleeping Earth!
Healthful and light, my Darling! may'st thou rise
With clear and chearful Eyes—
And of the same good Tidings to me send!   225
For oh! beloved Friend!
I am not the buoyant Thing I was of yore
When like an own Child, I to Joy belong'd:
For others mourning oft, myself oft sorely wrong'd,
Yet bearing all things then, as if I nothing bore!   230

Yes, dearest Sara, yes!
There *was* a time when tho' my path was rough,
The Joy within me dallied with Distress;
And all Misfortunes were but as the Stuff
Whence Fancy made me Dreams of Happiness;   235
For Hope grew round me, like the climbing Vine,
And Leaves and Fruitage, not my own, seem'd mine!
But now Ill Tidings bow me down to earth,
Nor care I that they rob me of my Mirth—
But oh! each Visitation   240
Suspends what Nature gave me at my Birth,
My shaping Spirit of Imagination!

I speak not now of those habitual Ills
That wear out Life, when two unequal Minds
Meet in one House and two discordant Wills—   245
    This leaves me, where it finds,

aloud, half in grief, and half in the hope of being heard by its
mother.'
221-2. These lines are quoted at the end of Coleridge's famous letter
about Sir Thomas Browne, 10 March 1804, thus:
        I trust that you are quietly asleep—and that
            all the stars hang bright above your dwelling
        Silent as tho' they watched the sleeping earth!
This letter has been printed as addressed to 'My dear—'; the manuscript reads 'My dear Sara'.

Past Cure, and past Complaint,—a fate austere
Too fix'd and hopeless to partake of Fear!

But thou, dear Sara! (dear indeed thou art,
My Comforter! a Heart within my Heart!)   250
Thou, and the Few, we love, tho' few ye be,
Make up a World of Hopes and Fears for me.
And if Affliction, or distemp'ring Pain,
Or wayward Chance befall you, I complain
Not that I mourn—O Friends, most dear! most true!   255
    Methinks to weep with you
Were better far than to rejoice alone—
But that my coarse domestic Life has known
No Habits of heart-nursing Sympathy,
No Griefs but such as dull and deaden me,   260
No mutual mild Enjoyments of it's own,
No Hopes of its own Vintage, None O! none—
Whence when I mourn'd for you, my Heart might borrow
Fair forms and living Motions for it's Sorrow.
For not to think of what I needs must feel,   265
But to be still and patient all I can;
And haply by abstruse Research to steal
From my own Nature, all the Natural man—
This was my sole Resource, my wisest plan!
And that, which suits a part, infects the whole,   270
And now is almost grown the Temper of my Soul.

My little Children are a Joy, a Love,
    A good Gift from above!
But what is Bliss, that still calls up a Woe,
    And makes it doubly keen   275
Compelling me to *feel*, as well as *know*,
What a most blessed Lot mine might have been.
Those little Angel Children (woe is me!)
There have been hours when feeling how they bind
And pluck out the Wing-feathers of my Mind,   280
Turning my Error to Necessity,
I have half-wish'd they never had been born!
That seldom! but sad Thoughts they always bring,
And like the Poet's Philomel, I sing
My Love-song, with my breast against a Thorn.   285

With no unthankful Spirit I confess,
This clinging Grief, too, in it's turn, awakes
That Love, and Father's Joy; but O! it makes
The Love the greater, and the Joy far less.
These Mountains too, these Vales, these Woods, these Lakes,
Scenes full of Beauty and of Loftiness   291
Where all my Life I fondly hop'd to live—
I were sunk low indeed, did they *no* solace give;
But oft I seem to feel, and evermore I fear,
They are not to me now the Things, which once they were.

O Sara! we receive but what we give,   296
And in *our* life alone does Nature live
Our's is her Wedding Garment, our's her Shroud—
And would we aught behold of higher Worth
Than that inanimate cold World allow'd   300
To the poor loveless ever anxious Crowd,
Ah! from the Soul itself must issue forth
A Light, a Glory, and a luminous Cloud
Enveloping the Earth!
And from the Soul itself must there be sent   305
A sweet and potent Voice, of it's own Birth,
Of all sweet Sounds, the Life and Element.
O pure of Heart! thou need'st not ask of me
What this strong music in the Soul may be,
What and wherein it doth exist,   310
This Light, this Glory, this fair luminous Mist,
This beautiful and beauty-making Power!
Joy, innocent Sara! Joy, that ne'er was given
Save to the Pure, and in their purest Hour,
Joy, Sara! is the Spirit and the Power,   315
That wedding Nature to us gives in Dower
    A new Earth and new Heaven,
Undreamt of by the Sensual and the Proud!
Joy is that strong Voice, Joy that luminous Cloud—
    We, we ourselves rejoice!   320
And thence flows all that charms or ear or sight,
All melodies, the Echoes of that Voice,
All Colors a Suffusion of that Light.

295. Cf. Wordsworth's *Ode*, l. 9: The things which I have seen I now
can see no more.

Sister and Friend of my devoutest Choice
Thou being innocent and full of love,   325
And nested with the Darlings of thy Love,
And feeling in thy Soul, Heart, Lips, and Arms
Even what the conjugal and mother Dove,
That borrows genial Warmth from those, she warms,
Feels in the thrill'd wings, blessedly outspread—   330
Thou free'd awhile from Cares and human Dread
By the Immenseness of the Good and Fair
   Which thou seest everywhere—
Thus, thus, should'st thou rejoice!
To thee would all things live from Pole to Pole;   335
Their Life the Eddying of thy living Soul—
O dear! O Innocent! O full of Love!
A very Friend! A Sister of my Choice—
O dear, as Light and Impulse from above,
Thus may'st thou ever, evermore rejoice!   340

                    S.T.C.

IV

LANDOR'S PROSE[1]

AMONG the masters of nineteenth-century literature Walter Savage Landor holds a distinguished
place. As a poet he was eclipsed by the five great
luminaries of the romantic revival, yet much of his
verse has a high excellence in its own original vein.
As a writer of prose none has surpassed him. If he
made no striking contribution to the development of
thought, he yet gave currency to the ripest wisdom and
the noblest reflections; and his imaginary portraits of
men and women of all ages are touched with a knowledge and sympathy which show him to have been
always at home with great thoughts and great men.
Throughout a long life his character and genius made
a deep impression upon his more notable contemporaries, from Wordsworth and Southey to Carlyle and
Dickens, Browning and Swinburne; and to-day, by the
few who know him, he is prized alike for the spacious-
ness of his thought and for the rare beauty and dignity
of his style. But to the wider public he is barely more
than a name; and there is probably no modern English
classic so little appreciated at his true worth.

The reasons are not far to seek. That proud independence of mind and character, which gives an in-
disputable grandeur to his life, brought him inevitably
into conflict with the tastes and opinions of the world.
'From my earliest years,' he wrote, 'I have avoided society as
much as I could decorously, for I received more pleasure from
the cultivation and improvement of my own thoughts than in
walking up and down among the thoughts of others. Yet I have
never avoided the intercourse of men distinguished by virtue
and genius; of genius because it warmed and invigorated me by

[1] The Introduction to Landor's *Imaginary Conversations* (World's
Classics, No. 196).

my trying to keep pace with it, of virtue that if I had any of my
own it might be called forth by such vicinity.'

Communing thus with his own thoughts, in intercourse
with his noble friends, and with the still nobler heroes
of the past, he could never attain to sympathy with
those who moved upon a lower level of intellect and
emotion. He walked 'upon the uplands, meditating and
remembering', and when summoned to the plains, on
which the mundane affairs of life are conducted by
ordinary men and women, his haughty but sensitive
nature was ill at ease. Generous to a fault, delicately
susceptible to all the finer feelings, courteous and
polished in demeanour, he was yet irritable and passionate, impatient of weakness or stupidity, quickly
roused to anger at real or imaginary wrong, and when
roused deeply resentful. His outer life was a series of
quarrels, for the most part arising from trivial causes,
but bitter enough in their effect upon his happiness, of
petty trials which his undisciplined nature rendered
intolerable. He was never able to accommodate himself to that world in which the man of genius, no less
than others, is called upon to live. He realized it himself; and many of his finest utterances may be regarded
as the calm comments of Landor the artist upon the
errors and the follies of Landor the man.

That same unyielding disposition which made him
difficult to live with has made him difficult to read.
He never courted popularity. 'I never ask the public
opinion of what I write,' he said. 'God forbid that
it should be favourable, for more people think in-
judiciously than judiciously.' This is not ingratiating.
It only differs from Ben Jonson's 'By God, 'tis good,
and if you like 't, you may' in that it accepts without
loss of temper the inevitable indifference of a despised
and flouted audience. Landor was content to appeal
to the few. But whilst he could never have been widely
popular, a closer touch with public opinion would have

extended the circle of his influence. It would, moreover, have done something to clear his art of two faults
which mar it even in the judgement of that high
tribunal whose verdict he sought. Two dangers beset
the writer who does not test his work by its effect upon
others. His own reflections, profound and trivial alike,
gain a special value for him, so that he is prone to
expatiate on petty crotchets or prejudices as though
they were eternal principles. On the other hand, when
his thought is vital and its development in his own
mind clear enough, he may give it a semblance of
obscurity by the suppression of necessary links in its
sequence. Both these faults Landor might have learned
to cure by a fuller sympathy with the public he
despised; and their correction would have entailed no
surrender of his independence and originality, but
merely the removal of obstructions which impeded his
just recognition.

Landor's outlook on life, his taste in art, and his
manner of utterance are alike his own. He is remote
from the literary current of his time. In an age when
romanticism was in full flood he kept steadily before
him the ideals and the temper of classic art. By the
ideas let loose upon the world at the French Revolution
he was as deeply moved as Wordsworth or as Shelley,
but from their realization he hoped not for a new
heaven and a new earth, but rather for a return to the
noblest traditions of Athens and of Rome. He was as
passionately idealistic as any poet or dreamer of the
day, and the art in which he sought both refuge and
expression was the product of hours of tense excitement, of deep emotional sympathy with his subject.
Yet it bears no traces of the throes of its creation;
its pervading characteristics are simplicity of design, a
careful finish in execution, and a serenity of spirit that
proclaims him its master and not its slave. The wide
field of subjects over which his writings range gives

evidence enough of breadth of reading, possible only to a long and leisured life. But whatever theme he handled he handled in the same severe manner. His intellectual and artistic sympathies were fixed in boyhood by a passion for classical antiquity which other interests could never shake.

At Rugby School he was famous as a brilliant Latin scholar, and throughout his life he wrote as fluently in Latin as in his mother tongue. As an old man he once said, 'I am sometimes at a loss for an English word, for a Latin, never.' There was much, indeed, as Carlyle noted, of the 'unsubduable old Roman' about Landor's character and outlook upon life; and his portraits of the heroes of the ancient Republic, both in their struggles and in their refined leisure—his Marcellus, his Scipio, his Lucullus—show the insight of a true humanist. And though his knowledge of the Greek language was less accurate, his sympathy with Greek life and culture was as constant and as profound. In the world of her beautiful mythology, in Periclean Athens, in the idyllic scenes of Theocritus, he was equally at home; and Hellenic ideals of art and of life had a reality to him which not only gave him the power to embody them without the intrusion of modern sentiment, but enabled him to handle modern themes in something of their spirit. His proud assertion

> I write as others wrote
> On Sunium's height

was no empty boast.

The direction given to Landor's thought and tastes by his study of the classics was enhanced by a lifelong devotion to Milton, that modern who alone rivalled them in his affections, and rivalled them because he partook so largely of their salient qualities. 'My prejudices in favour of ancient literature began to wear away on reading *Paradise Lost*, and even the great hexameter sounded to me tinkling when I had recited aloud, in my solitary walks upon the seashore, the haughty appeal of Satan, and the repentance of Eve.' Yet to Landor Milton was greater than his art. In Milton he saw one of the sublime characters of the world; and some of his noblest writing is devoted to praise of his hero's superb idealism, his fearless, independent republicanism, his passionate devotion to the cause of liberty and of truth. As far as Landor could be said to have one model upon whose image he moulded his life and thought, that model was Milton. For Milton's political career, to many of his readers a stumbling-block and to the mere aesthetic critic foolishness, Landor had nothing but eulogy; and Milton's attacks upon hypocrisy, fraud, and priestcraft re-echo in the *Imaginary Conversations*. 'Give me the liberty to know, to utter, and to argue freely, according to conscience, above all liberties,' is the cry in which Milton gives voice to the root passion of his life. Similarly, Landor asserts that the purpose of all his writing, as far as it has a purpose extrinsic of pure art, is to advocate freedom of thought, or, as he picturesquely puts it, 'to remove and consume the gallows which await the independent thinker in any branch of human activity'.

Many of his leading ideas were connected with this passion for liberty and for independence: many of his heroes—Pericles, Demosthenes, Metellus, Washington, Hofer, Kościuszko—those whose lives were kindled to a like passion. His consistent hatred of monarchy sprang from the notion that it must tend to suppress the free development of the individual. 'Men, like trees,' he said, 'acquire robustness and nobility by standing separately. Princes are so educated as to detest the unmalleable honesty which will receive no impression from them, nor do they let you serve them unless they can bend you double.' But his republicanism, like Milton's, saw in democracy as fatal a tyranny as in kingship. It was essentially aristocratic. It desired the rule of the best. And like Milton's, too, it was necessarily independent of party. For the party man Landor had always a supreme contempt. 'He who declares himself a party man', he said, 'is a registered and enlisted slave. He begins by being a zealot, he ends by being a dupe.' In the reaction which followed the French Revolution he could oppose with determined hatred the different attempts throughout Europe to reinstate despotic governments, could support with enthusiasm all risings of nations striving for independence. He 'loved liberal measures, liberal institutions, liberal men, wherever they were to be found', but he could never ally himself with those who wished to put fuller political power into the hands of the people.

He called himself a Conservative. He 'would alter little, but correct much'. But he was really an isolated idealist, lifting up his voice for liberty and for a higher tone in national and political thinking. If this independence of party limited his practical influence, at least it kept him faithful to that revolutionary creed upon which Wordsworth and Coleridge, with so many of his peers, turned nervously apologetic backs. And his general reflections are fully as inspiring and suggestive as theirs, with as clear a value for us to-day. Thus he places ambition among the most dangerous of political vices. 'God sometimes sends a famine, sometimes a hero, for the chastisement of mankind.' And he speaks in a fine scorn of the jealousy with which one nation is apt to view its neighbour's prosperity— 'a prosperity raised by her industry, by the honesty of her dealings, by excelling us in the quality of her commodity, in the exactness of her workmanship, in punctuality, and in credit'. As for the incitement of war on such grounds,

'Hell itself,' he exclaims, 'with all its jealousy and malignity and falsehood, could not utter a sentence more pernicious to the

interests of mankind. It is the duty of every state to provide
and watch that no other lose an inch of territory or a farthing
of wealth by aggression. Correct your own habits and you need
not fear your rivals. The aggrandisement of a neighbour is no
detriment to us. If we are honest and industrious his wealth is
ours.'

Lofty as was the plane from which Landor judged
human affairs, he was constitutionally averse to all
thought which had no practical bearing upon daily
life. The sanity, the lucidity, the reserve which seemed
to him to be of the very essence of Greek temper made
him suspicious of any tendency towards mysticism.
For those who

> reasoned high
> Of providence, foreknowledge, will, and fate,
> Fix'd fate, free will, foreknowledge absolute,
> And found no end, in wandering mazes lost,

he felt a truly Miltonic contempt. This was not because
his own conceptions were materialistic, but because he
was content to leave alone those matters on which no
certainty could be attained, from whose discussion he
saw no result save a loss of charity and self-control.
'I hold it', he said, 'the most unphilosophical thing in
the world to call away men from useful occupations
and mutual help to profitless speculations and arid
controversies.' Hence sprang his rooted dislike to
Plato. Plato's subtle dialectics seemed to him a barren
linguistic trickery, and his imaginative reaching after
a truth that could never be defined, an occupation
essentially un-Hellenic. Landor understood and appreciated the genius of Plato no better than the average
Athenian must have done. In a long dialogue, of high
value despite its travesty of the greatest thinker of the
ancient world, Plato is put before us as a conceited and
self-seeking sophist, routed at every turn of the argument by Diogenes, the true philosopher, whose mind
is wholly set upon the search for practical truth. 'The

bird of wisdom flies low, and seeks her food under
hedges: the eagle himself would be starved if he always
soared aloft and against the sun.'

Where all his greater contemporaries were conscious
or unconscious Platonists, Landor kept his feet planted
firmly upon earth. 'The best sight', he said, 'is not that
which sees best in the twilight'; and again, 'To see
distant things better than near is a clear proof of defec-
tive sight.' He would have agreed with the modern
critic of Maeterlinck that, after all, the temple of
mysticism is situated in the same street as the cave of
Adullam. Yet the calm and the courage of spirit with
which he confronts human destiny has something in
common with the supreme triumphs of transcendental
experience; and they render the same tribute to 'that
soul which is the eternity of thought'. Of old age, he
writes: 'Let us yield to it, just as season yields to season,
hour to hour, and with a bright serenity, such as Evening is invested with by the departing Sun.' And he lays
to rest the terrors of death with the sublime reflection,
'What if it makes our enemies cease to hate us, what
if it makes our friends love us more!' Here are no
obstinate questionings, no blank misgivings, but rather
the steady clear-eyed vision of a man who 'knows what
life and death is', and who, schooled to the temper of
calm acceptance, cherishes every breath of the beauty
and fragrance of life. Hence Epicurus was the philosopher who had for him the deepest attraction; and the
discourse which Epicurus holds with his young friends
Leontion and Ternissa was his favourite among the
Imaginary Conversations. The Epicurus whom he presents is not the apostle of what is falsely called epi-
cureanism—a perversion, like all popular conceptions
of religion, of the ideas of its founder—but rather the
Epicurus of history idealized, accepting the joys of
nature and life which come in his path, refusing to be
disturbed by angry threats of enraged neglected deities,

joyfully taking the benefit that comes spontaneously, 'wishing no more for what is a hair's breadth beyond our reach than for a draught of water from the Ganges', and, because he lives so, fearing nothing from a future life.

The same dominant ideas are developed in his writing upon religion and in his studies of the religious character. He has little sympathy with the mystic, and for the theological dialectician or controversialist nothing but contempt; but his appreciation of the simple religious nature whose faith is shown in works is both full and subtle. For Dante as poet and as man he had full admiration, but for the characteristic thought of Dante no more understanding than he showed for Plato: the genius of medieval Italy was summed up for him in the essentially human, sunny, unmedieval Boccaccio. It is significant that in his conception of Joan of Arc there is no allusion to those mystic relations with the unseen with which medieval superstition invested her. She is simply the maid of action and of self-renunciation, and is presented to us in contrast with Agnès Sorel, the king's mistress, who has all the externals of religious faith without the character to give them reality.

Agnes. But if the saints of heaven are offended, it would be presumptuous in the king to expose his person in battle, until we have supplicated and appeased them.

Jeanne. One hour of self-denial, one hour of stern exertion against the assault of passion, outvalues a life of prayer.

Agnes. Prayer, if many others will pray with us, can do all things. . . . I will throw myself on the pavement, and pray until no star is in the heavens. Oh! I will so pray, so weep.

Jeanne. Unless you save the tears of others, in vain you shed your own.

Agnes. Again I ask you, what *can* I do?

Jeanne. When God has told you what you ought to do, he has already told you what you can.

Landor judged of religion by its practical and vital

force. 'The good citizen and the calm reasoner come
at once to the same conclusion: that philosophy can
never hold many men together; that religion can; and
those who are without it would not let philosophy, nor
law, nor humanity exist. Therefore', he urges, 'it is our
duty and interest to remove all obstruction from it, to
give it light, air, space, and freedom.'

'Light, air, space, freedom', these are in Landor's
eyes essential to healthy spiritual growth. Hence his
impatience both of superstition and of persecution.
The darker side of Roman Catholicism has never been
more ruthlessly exposed than in his portraits of Louis
XIV and Father La Chaise; he often takes it as a type
of all that is venal, tyrannical, and mystifying in religion.
But such vices are not the monopoly of one Church.
Calvin has as much to answer for as any Pope. 'Even
if our country is not Roman Catholic,' he says, 'we all
live under a kind of popish government. There are
popes in all creeds, in all countries, in all ages.' And
wherever intolerance is found, freedom of thought
suffers. The dialogue between Melanchthon and Calvin
is chiefly devoted to the contrast between the inexo-
rable dogmatist who would force his opinions down the
throats of his fellow creatures and the true Christian
who, deprecating controversy, preaches a larger charity.
'I remember', says Melanchthon, 'no discussion of religion in which religion was not a sufferer by it, if
mutual forbearance and belief in another's good motives
and intentions are (as I must always think they are) its
proper and necessary appurtenances.' Upon outward
observances he lays small store.

'Religion is too pure for corporations; it is best meditated on in
privacy, and best acted on in ordinary intercourse with mankind. If we believe in revelation we must believe that God
wishes us to converse with Him but little, since the only form
of address He has presented to us is an extremely short one.
He has placed us where our time may be more beneficially

employed in mutually kind offices. Articles of faith are innocent in themselves, but upon articles of faith what incontrollable domination, what insupportable prerogatives, what insolent frauds, have been asserted and enforced. I am ready to be of that church which has the fewest of them.'

And high among the Christian virtues Landor places the duty of cheerfulness. 'Be assured', says Boccaccio, in whose mouth he puts many of his most deeply felt beliefs, 'our heavenly Father is as well pleased to see His children in the playground as in the school-room. He has provided both for us.' And again,

'I devoutly hold to the sacrament and the mysteries—yet somehow I would rather see men tranquillized than frightened out of their senses, and rather fast asleep than burning. Sometimes I have been ready to believe, as far as our holy faith will allow me, that it were better our Lord were nowhere, than torturing in His inscrutable wisdom, to all eternity, so many myriads of us poor devils, the creatures of His hands. . . . I would be a good Catholic, alive or dead. But, upon my conscience, it goes hard with me to think it of Him, when I hear that woodlark yonder gushing with joyousness, or when I see the beautiful clouds, resting so softly one upon another, dissolving—and not damned for it.'

Such is the character of the thought that Landor scatters in profusion throughout his writings. Hardly a page is without its memorable words, not flaunted to dazzle the reader, nor fondled as though their author was loath to part with them, but cast from him with secure and easy mastery. 'Thought', he writes, 'is never thrown away: wherever it falls, or runs, or rests, it fertilizes.' Open our Landor where we will, we cannot read far before we meet some wise saw, some striking image, that arrests the attention and sets the mind working; whilst if we light upon one of the many best passages, it will go hard with us to match its power to brace the intellect and ennoble the heart. There may be nothing new in the ideas that Landor presents: the

originality is rather in the man than in his ideas, in
their emotional value rather than in their intellectual
content. It is the function of the artist not so much to
discover truth as to make it current. There is little
truth that familiarity has not degraded to the commonplace; and the minor artist, in despair of material so
unpromising as truth, is tempted into paradox. 'Paradox', as Landor tells us, 'is dear to most people: it
bears the appearance of originality, but it is usually the
talent of the superficial, the perverse, and the obstinate':
it is the glory of artistic genius to quicken the commonplace and reinstate it once more as vital truth. This is
Landor's achievement. Schooled by the greatest masters,
he yet accepts nothing at second hand. He is always
independent, always sincere. The application of his
ideas to particular persons and situations may at times
be prejudiced enough: in generalization he is always
great, stamping on his utterances the impress of a noble
and distinguished personality, and by the felicity of
their phrasing and the wealth of their imaginative
colour giving them life, and beauty, and fertilizing
power.

   Landor's literary reputation rests most securely upon
his prose. But though he realized from the first that
prose was his 'study and business', he was in no hurry
to establish his pre-eminence. He was a poet of rare
distinction, if not of fame, at twenty-five years old; he
was nearly fifty when, in 1824, he produced the first
series of his *Imaginary Conversations*. 'All strong and
generous wine', he tells us, 'must deposit its crust before
it gratifies the palate', and in his earlier prose, discur-
sively critical of politics, literature, and society, still
more perhaps in his verse, his experience of life and
his command over the resources of language can alike
be seen attaining to mellowness and maturity. The
Imaginary Conversation was a form of art most clearly
suited to bring out the best elements in his genius and

to minimize the worst. He had not that feeling for construction, that supple, quick-moving style, necessary to a writer of good narrative or complete drama. When he takes upon himself to tell a story in prose he often tells it badly; when he should keep to one point he is liable to wander from it. A striking image, a stirring reflection such as may come to him at any moment from some side-light upon his subject, is apt, when the emotion is not tense, to take him off his chosen track into some alluring by-way. But such is the way of conversation, which is most fruitful when its course is least rigorously controlled. Landor loved dialogue for its 'facility of turning the cycle of our thoughts to whatever aspect we wish'. Moreover, it responded to a distinctive quality in his genius. He was constitutionally incapable of clear abstract thinking; but when, in the manner of the dramatist, he could merge his personality in that of other men, thoughts would flash upon him, like sparks struck out, from the contact of mind with mind, of character with character. 'It has always appeared to me', he says, 'that conversation brings forth ideas readily and plenteously, and that the ideas of one person no sooner come out than another's follow them, whether upon the same side or the opposite.' Landor drew out his own thoughts upon the same principle. And he delighted to justify his method by precedent. 'The best writers of every age', he reminds us, 'have written in dialogue: the best parts of Homer and Milton are speeches and replies: the best parts of the great historians are the same: the wisest men of Athens and of Rome converse together in this manner, as they are shown to us by Xenophon, by Plato, and by Cicero.' And to this method he remained faithful. To the *Imaginary Conversations* he added throughout the rest of his life, till they numbered one hundred and fifty. Of his other prose writings, *The Citation of William Shakespeare* and the *Pentameron* are protracted dialogues with narrative interspersed, and *Pericles and Aspasia* was composed in the form of intimate and intimately connected letters which, like all correspondence worthy of the name, are of the nature of conversation conducted from a distance.

The range of characters whom Landor reveals, and through whom he reveals himself, is unrivalled by any other author. Most felicitous, perhaps, in his delineation of ancient Greece and Rome, of the Italy of the Renaissance, and of his native land from Plantagenet times down to his own day, he hardly leaves a country or a civilization unrepresented in his gallery of illustrious portraits. 'The noble mansion', he held, 'is most distinguished by the beautiful images it retains of beings passed away, and so is the noble mind.' With the heroes of the past he loved to commune in that solitude that was to him best society.

'Among the chief pleasures of my life,' he tells us, 'and among the commonest of my occupations, was the bringing before me such heroes and heroines of antiquity, such poets and sages, such of the prosperous and unfortunate, as most interested me by their courage, their eloquence, or their adventures. Engaging them in the conversations best suited to their characters, I knew perfectly their manners, their steps, their voices, and often did I moisten with my tears the models I had been forming of the less happy.'

Thus his imagination was able to call them from the shades, and see them in their habit as they lived; to him, as to Wordsworth, there was

> One great society alone on earth,
> The noble living and the noble dead.

History was to Landor a succession of vivid personalities, whose actions and whose thoughts revealed not only themselves, but the characteristics of the time which produced them. To know them was to know their age. In his presentation of them he was quite careless of historical accuracy, of date, place, or situation. He is full of anachronisms and discrepancies in literal fact. It was not the letter but the spirit as he conceived it that he wished to reproduce, and he felt quite free to take any liberties with historical fact which tended to bring out the essential qualities of his dramatis personae. For he was artist primarily, not historian. Thus, in a conversation of exquisite beauty, *The Lady Lisle and Elizabeth Gaunt*, two heroic women judicially murdered by Judge Jeffreys for harbouring rebels are brought together by Landor in the hour before their execution. As a matter of fact they never met. But the fiction is justified by the opportunity it affords for revealing to us the inner springs of their natures. And similarly, in no way could the character of Catharine of Russia be more vividly presented to us than at the very moment when the murder of her husband, long and eagerly planned, is at last executed, and when in transports of suppressed excitement she stands with her more timid confidante at the door of the palace, and hears his blood dripping upon the floor, and the patter of the dogs' feet as they carry the marks over the palace stairs. To this dialogue Landor added a note significant beyond its actual context. 'It is unnecessary to inform the generality of readers that Catharine was not present at the murder of her husband. Nor is it easy to believe that Clytemnestra was at the murder of hers. Our business (i.e. the business of Aeschylus and all true dramatic writers) is character.' His practice is the same when his object is less obviously dramatic, and his conversation interesting rather from its ideas than from the tensity of the situation. Thus Bacon talks with Hooker at a date when Hooker had already been in the grave some ten years. Machiavelli refers to the Spanish Armada and the wars in the Netherlands. Landor does not even scruple to put into the mouths of Greeks or Romans allusions to characters and events of his own day. But he is always true to his conception of character and nationality, representing in his dramatis personae those qualities in which, as it seemed to him, not only the individuality of the speaker, but also the genius of his nation and the peculiar spirit of his age, found clear and forcible illustration.

For his discursive dialogues he selects characters from all epochs of history, who represent ideas sympathetic with his own, either pitted against antagonists whose opposition places them in high relief, or in converse with those whose friendly understanding can elicit their most intimate reflections. Thus, as we have seen, Epicurus discourses with his friends, whereas Diogenes engages in dialectic with his adversary. Similarly, Epictetus reveals his simple sincerity in contrast with the worldly minded Seneca; the sweet reasonableness of Melanchthon's Christianity is contrasted with Calvin's domineering and dogmatic intolerance; and Marvell sings the praises and defends the honour of Milton to the deprecating time-server, Bishop Parker: whereas Marcus Cicero converses of philosophy with his brother Quinctus on the eve of his last birthday; Barrow gives wise counsel to his young pupil Newton; and Washington and Franklin discourse of liberty and of the future of America and England. In the shorter, more dramatic conversations, Landor displays in active exercise those virtues and vices which have formed the theme of his more discursive dialogues. Superstition, and cruelty, its constant ally, are exposed with a ferocious humour in the broad comedy of his *Louis XIV and Father La Chaise*, in a lighter satiric spirit the economies and the diplomatic deceits of Queen Elizabeth are exhibited in her conversations with her sister, with Cecil, and with her French suitor; whilst occasionally, as in the delicate portraiture of the Duchesse de Fontanges, the foibles of his victim are touched with so light a hand as barely to affect the charm of the character portrayed.

But Landor is most successful with characters of more

heroic build, pre-eminent either in noble action or in
their capacity for suffering, great by a courage that is
not merely physical, but is the index of moral and
spiritual grandeur—by love that triumphs even in its
apparent defeat, or by that submission to cruel destiny
or unjust doom which is a proof not of man's cowering
will, but of his unconquerable mind. Like the true
classic artist in his outlook upon life, he is always
arrested by the greatness of the soul of man. His
modern sentiment is revealed by the larger emphasis
he lays upon the element of tenderness with which for
him greatness is ever associated. Of what passes in the
world for greatness—the power of a tyrant with brutal
lusts or low selfish desires—he has given many pictures;
but bold and striking as they are, they tend to be exaggerated, and lack the true psychological insight with
which he penetrates into those whom he can view with
less bias. They are indeed dangerously like stage tyrants.
Such characters, though they dominate the stage on
which they act, as indeed they dominate the stage of
life, are of interest to Landor chiefly as dramatic foils.
Thus, Peter the Great, with his total lack of natural
human feeling, throws into relief his highly strung,
susceptible son, Alexis, who is swayed by emotions and
inspired by ideals incomprehensible to his father, and
yearns for a love of which his brutal parent is wholly
incapable. In a scene conceived on similar lines,
Henry VIII visits Anne Boleyn on the night before
her execution. He is half-drunk, and wholly oblivious
of her tender love for him and for her child—now
boisterously jocose, now hurling at her shameful charges
which he half-knows to be false. He laughs at her
memories of a happier past, and taunts her as she pleads
not for forgiveness for what she has not committed, but
rather for some return of the Henry that she still loves.
These portraits of Peter and of Henry are undoubtedly
overdrawn, but their very exaggeration serves an obvious

artistic purpose. It strengthens our sense of pathos at
the sight of an exquisite fragile beauty, 'beauty that is
no stronger than a flower', trodden under a wanton and
muddy heel. Landor's hatred of cruelty and tyranny
was such that his art was sometimes at its mercy: in
dealing with them alone does he seem to forget that
classical maxim, μηδὲν ἄγαν, to which, as a rule, he
adhered with bare severity. Not a few critics have felt
that Peter's voracious appetite on hearing of his son's
death is over-emphasized, and would have preferred,
at least, the omission from his menu of the 'caviare and
good strong cheese'. But Landor's real interest in these
two dialogues is centred in Alexis and in Anne Boleyn.
He delighted to delineate those rare and delicate souls,
of whom it might be said that

injuries

Made them more gracious, and their nature then
Did breathe its sweetness out most sensibly,
As aromatic flowers on Alpine turf,
When foot hath crushed them.

Landor's art is at its finest when his characters are
less fiercely contrasted, and when the tyrant has some
redeeming qualities, even if he is incapable of entering
into the subtler emotions of the heroine. So it is in
Leofric and Godiva, perhaps Landor's most famous
dialogue, as it was certainly among his own favourites.
Leofric's love, after its own boisterous fashion, is perfectly genuine, and we are made to feel that through
it his redemption may ultimately come; but at present
it is entirely selfish, and thrives by the side of a callous
indifference to the suffering and the starvation of his
thralls. There is nothing exaggerated, nothing even
unusual in the character, yet its contrast is vivid enough
with the sublime figure of Godiva, whose newly
awakened love for her lord has awakened also all the
finer possibilities of her being. It is inseparable from
her joy in the beauty of nature—'Sad is the day, and

worse must follow, when we hear the blackbird in the garden and do not throb with joy'—it quickens, instead of stifling, her sympathy with the poorest of her subjects, and inspires her to an act of self-sacrifice in which she stakes more than life itself.

It is indeed to be noted that the closer the sympathy between the characters presented, the subtler is Landor's presentation of them and the more delicate his psychological insight. So it is in the scene already referred to between The Lady Lisle and Elizabeth Gaunt, so in that magnificent colloquy upon the battlefield between Marcellus, the dying Roman, and Hannibal, his Carthaginian conqueror. Their rival states are in a death-struggle for supremacy; yet the patriotism which has made them mortal enemies does not prevent either from appreciating the nobility of the other. In Hannibal is finely delineated the conflict between exultation at his victory and admiration for the fallen Roman, for whom he shows an almost tender chivalry. 'Send a vessel off to Carthage. Say Hannibal is at the gates of Rome—Marcellus, who stood alone between us, fallen. Brave man! I would rejoice, and cannot. How awfully serene a countenance! And how glorious a form and stature! And what plain armour!' And in the few words of Marcellus those qualities shine out to which the Roman Republic owed its greatness and its glory—courage, simplicity, love of home, passionate pride in the city for which, even in its utter danger, he will not counsel submission.

If scenes like these are to yield up to us their full secret, they must be read not with the eye alone, but with an intensity of thought and feeling sufficient to call them up before our minds alive and moving as Landor saw them. Their high artistic concentration can only appeal to the reader whose imagination is awake to their central emotion, and is readily responsive to the subtle transitions of feeling through which the characters pass. They are classical, not only in their reserve and in their emphasis upon the heroic in character and situation, but also in a certain statuesque quality in their conception. Lessing, in his treatise on the Laocoön, has pointed out that 'the artist who aims at presenting one moment and one aspect of it, as does the sculptor or the painter, cannot be too careful that the moment and aspect chosen shall be in the highest degree pregnant in its meaning—that is, shall yield the utmost range to the activities of the imagination'. Some might conceive that the moment to be chosen would be the climax.

'But', says Lessing, 'in the whole evolution of the passion there is no one stage which has less of this advantage than its highest. Beyond it there is nothing, and to present the last extremity to the eye is in effect to put fetters on the imagination, and by denying it all possibility of rising above the sensible impression presented by the artist, to throw its activities forcibly on the weaker images that lie below that impression.'

In the *Imaginary Conversations*, which offer scenes chosen as it were from unwritten dramas, Landor's artistic instinct guides him to follow this principle. The moment that he delights in depicting is that preceding the climax of the action, when some great resolution has been taken, but has yet to be fulfilled, as in the *Leofric and Godiva*, or when, as with Catharine of Russia, some great action long planned has at last been executed, and now that the climax is over, the character, as it were, recoils upon itself, and is revealed in all its complexity. He is at his greatest when some heroic soul is faced with death, and, freed at last from the trivialities that tended to obscure its true proportions, it stands out in clear outline, the light of eternity behind it. Landor does not present the death, but what might be called the emotional pose that precedes it. But in every case what he exhibits is some pause in the action, a moment when nothing is done, but much has to be endured. And in this moment of tragic suspense we feel, as it were by contrast, the passionate storm of life from which for an instant the actors have emerged. The action is all about us, through our own lively sense of the immediate past or the immediate future; it is present with us in the cries of battle which die away into the distance as we listen to the last words of Marcellus to Hannibal, in the forebodings of Godiva when the people crowd about her as she enters the city on the eve of her sacrifice—'I hope they will not crowd about me so to-morrow.' But the scene before us has the impressive stillness of arrested movement, giving opportunity for that revelation of spirit which in the tumult of action would escape observation. It is the supreme function of Landor's art, like that of painting or of sculpture, to give

> To one brief moment caught from fleeting time
> The appropriate calm of blest Eternity.

The attainment of this effect depends no more upon the careful choice of the scene to be presented than upon the manner of its presentation. Landor never gives a full statement, he never exhausts his emotion; he leaves much to be overheard by sensitive ears, relying throughout upon his elaborate and studied use of literary irony. Of irony, in the popular sense of the word, Landor was a master, and his satire is most effective, either when it is Socratic, or when he puts into the mouth of his characters words which, unconsciously to them, reveal to us their own weaknesses. But literary irony is put to higher purpose than satire. It is based not so much on the different construction put upon words by their speaker and by their audience as upon the general inadequacy of words altogether to express what we wish them to convey. Like all successful devices of art, it has its foundation in nature and the experience of life. Every man knows that when he feels

most acutely he says the least, and that little not always
to the point, and also that in moments of great stress,
in crises of action or of feeling, conversation is definitely
pitched in a low key. The artist realizes it, and conscious that however masterly his command of language,
it yet fails before the infinite possibilities of the human
spirit, he significantly refuses, at times, to get as near as
he can to expression, and has recourse to deliberate
understatement. By pointed omission, or by reference
to some triviality that seems to call us away from the
central passion that is throbbing in us, he rouses our
sense of inadequacy or incongruity, thus concentrating
us all the more poignantly upon the reality.

Even the great romantic artists, whose aim for the
most part is the height of expression, fall back, in the
last resource, upon the ironic method. Telling strokes
of it are to be found in Othello's last great utterance,
perhaps the finest dramatic speech in literature, and
the dying words of Webster's Duchess are wholly conceived in this manner:

> I pray thee, look thou give my little boy
> Some syrup for his cold, and let the girl
> Say her prayers, ere she sleep.

Much of Landor's art depends upon an irony of this
kind, which he employs not merely for the climax, but
as a continual and studied means to restrain any undue
outburst of emotion. Thus it is in his conversation
between Leonora di Este and the Cardinal Panigarola.
The hapless love of the poet Tasso and the Princess
Leonora di Este, and Tasso's imprisonment by her
tyrannical brother on the charge of madness, is a story
of sure appeal to Landor. The scene in which he has
chosen to depict it is that where Leonora, on her death-
bed, receives from her confessor the last tidings of her
lover. In order to appreciate its delicacy, we must bear
in mind that Tasso, spied upon even in prison, has not

dared to speak to the priest of the passion that devours him, nor dare the priest convey from him a direct message, and the irony of the situation is that the priest professes rather to prepare Leonora for her death than to encourage or satisfy her hopeless love. So throughout he pretends to interpret the words of Tasso and Leonora in a very different sense from that which they really suggest.

Leonora. I am prepared to depart, for I have struggled (God knows) to surmount what is unsurmountable. . . . Pray, father, for my deliverance; pray also for poor Torquato's: do not separate us in your prayers. O! could he leave his prison as surely and as speedily as I shall mine! it would not be more thankfully. O! that bars of iron were as fragile as bars of clay! O! that princes were as merciful as Death! But tell him, tell Torquato—go again; entreat, persuade, command him, to forget me.

Panigarola. Alas! even the command, even the command from you and from above, might not avail perhaps. You smile, Madonna!

Leonora. I die happy.

The whole brief dialogue, wherein little is stated but everything is conveyed, reveals in the subtlest and most delicate art the tragedy of Tasso and Leonora. And we feel its beauty and its pathos far more deeply than if every ounce of passion had been wrung from it by a consummate master of romance.

In the style of his *Imaginary Conversations* there is no attempt at dramatic realism. All the dramatis personae speak Landorian English, which is far different both in rhythm and structure from the language of ordinary conversation. Landor justifies this, as was his wont, by analogy with the practice of the greatest dramatic writers.

'No man in pain', he says, 'ever used the best part of the language used by Sophocles in his delineation of Philoctetes. We admit it, and willingly; and are at least as much illuded by it as

by anything else we hear or see upon the stage. Poets and
statuaries and painters give us an adorned imitation of the
object, so skilfully treated that we receive it for a correct one.
This is the only illusion that they aim at; this is the perfection
of their arts.'

Now, in verse dialogue most people are prepared to
accept this as a recognized artistic convention. They
do not call *Hamlet* unnatural because in real life Hamlet
would not have spoken in blank verse. They judge of
the language by its adequacy to express the ideas and
emotions of the speaker, and recognize that through
the beauty of the words they are attuned to sympathy
with his emotion. The music of Landor's prose, as
different from ordinary speech as that of Shakespeare's
verse, is employed by him for the same purpose. It has
its own beauty, beauty of a kind that creates the atmosphere in which his scenes have been conceived. Landor's
prose is careless of what is falsely called realism. It is
in 'the grand style', which arises here, as in poetry,
when a serious subject is treated 'with simplicity and
severity'. For if the object of art be to give immortality
to great human passion, if it is its function to make

> Sorrow more beautiful than beauty's self,

it can best be achieved by some kind of idealization,
and in a form which lowers that element that is painful and distressing in order to emphasize the hidden
emotion of which the physical is often an imperfect
manifestation. Few persons are beautiful when they
weep, none when they cry, however noble the emotion
that prompts their tears; and a realism that attempts
to represent their emotion by drawing the actual physical expression is doomed to irretrievable failure. Art
can depict satisfactorily by realistic methods the face
of the child that cries for chocolate: only by idealization
can it depict the face of the child that has lost its
mother. The truth that art aims at is not in the

external ugliness of the face in pain, whether physical
or mental, but in the essential beauty or greatness of the
emotion that sways it, and the imaginative sympathy with
that emotion which it is able to arouse in us; and it is to
awaken this and make us share it that the artist strives.

In that emotional prose which never overreaches
itself, yet has a beauty of melody and rhythm comparable to great poetry, Landor is one of our supreme
masters. Prose, he said, may be infinitely varied in
modulation, it is an extension of metres, an amplifica-
tion of harmonies, of which even the best and most
varied poetry admits but few; certainly his own prose
has a more varied and a subtler cadence than his verse.
But this does not imply either that he indulged in
extraneous ornament, or that he over-emphasized
musical effect. The first duty of a writer, he tells us, is
to be clear and concise. Obscurity is the worst fault in
writing—worse to him than a flaw in the grammar, 'for
we may discover a truth through such a defect which
we cannot through an obscurity'. And when he is
obscure himself, it is because of transitions too abrupt,
through over-conciseness—never through a lack of
clearness in his own mind. Next to lucidity, he delighted in fullness of sound and sense. It has often been
thought that his vocabulary is too much Latinized, but
though he loved Latin words for their sonority he used
none that had not been fully anglicized. In diction he
is always conservative, and speaks his word against slang
or slovenly attempts at picturesqueness of phrase. His
English is that of a scholar, but it is never pedantic, it
remains essentially English in idiom and in lucidity.
And the harmony of cadence that he gives it is not far-
sought at the expense of the logical or intellectual elements in the style. It is the blending of proportion and
force. 'Natural sequences and right subordination of
thoughts and that just proportion of numbers in the
sentences which follow a strong conception, are the

constituents of a true harmony.' And again, 'Whatever
is rightly said, sounds rightly.' His desire for a fullness
of sense as well as sound makes him an intensely
pictorial and imaginative writer. He often speaks in
metaphor. But metaphor with him is not ornament,
it is illumination. It arises inevitably from his artistic
conception of his subject. 'Never look abroad for
ornament' is his advice. 'Apollo, either as the god of
day or the slayer of the Python, had nothing to obscure
his clearness or impede his strength.' Many writers use
simile and metaphor either because they do not see
clearly or because they see double, because they cannot
express their meaning in plain language and strive to
hide their confusion of thought in a heap of glowing
words. Landor is poetic in style when he sees a thing
imaginatively, when his appeal is to the emotions as
well as to the intellect.

Of the beauty of his cadence and modulation, its
tender grace and restrained strength, examples will be
found in passages that I have already quoted. Whilst
it rarely encroaches upon the sphere of verse-rhythm,
it is as delicate and its appeal is as sure. Always measured
and serene, it rises with the emotion of the subject.
What could be more lovely in cadence and phrasing
than the words of Aesop to Rhodope?

'Laodameia died; Helen died; Leda, the beloved of Jupiter,
went before. It is better to repose in the earth betimes than to
sit up late; better, than to cling pertinaciously to what we feel
crumbling under us, and to protract an inevitable fall. We may
enjoy the present while we are insensible of infirmity and decay;
but the present, like a note in music, is nothing but as it apper-
tains to what is past and what is to come. There are no fields
of amaranth on this side of the grave: there are no voices, O
Rhodope, that are not soon mute, however tuneful: there is no
name, with whatever emphasis of passionate love repeated, of
which the echo is not faint at last.'

And in simple lucid prose Landor could attain

imaginative effects after which the more lyrical prose
romanticists strove, often in vain, with an elaborate
magnificence, or a strangeness of phrase and cadence
approximating to the style of poetry. This is best
exemplified in the three allegories, *Apologue of Critobulus*,
The Dream of Boccaccio, and *The Dream of Petrarca*.
Allegory was a form of art which Landor held in no
high esteem. It seemed to him a foggy way of presenting what ought to be presented clearly. He saw
how most allegorists either think too much of their
meaning and spoil their artistic picture, or think too
much of their picture and put in details that are
irrelevant to their meaning. But these short fables of
Landor's are among the few perfect allegories in the
language, each of them artistically beautiful, and yet
with every detail of the presentation adding force and
vividness to the truth he would present.

The limitations of Landor's art will be obvious
enough, and I have already touched upon them. He
exacts a heavy tax from his readers, assuming that they
will bring to their reading a greater knowledge of his
dramatis personae and their circumstances than can
fairly be expected, whilst the very clearness with which
he saw them imaged in his own mind, in their movements and gestures, and in the expression on their
countenances, often prevented him from leaving a sufficient clue by which we can follow his drift. At his best
he demands much concentration from us; and when he
is not at his best he lacks the supreme Hellenic quality
of clarity. It is true of him, as of all great writers, that
we must read him many times before his full meaning
reaches us; it is true also, that for even an attentive
mind the first reading is not so fruitful as it should be.
And his style and method, suited as it is to present the
heroic, the tender, and the pathetic—for all indeed
that moves upon clear and simple lines—is unfitted
to present the more complex and the evanescent. An

uncontrollable passion, a rapid interchange of emotion, are as much outside his scope as are all the lighter forms of comedy. His art could have fashioned a Desdemona but not an Othello, a Lady Macbeth but not a Cleopatra, a Perdita or Miranda but not a Beatrice or a Rosalind. His style, always graceful and dignified, often majestic, often tender, is not flexible, and when it trespasses beyond its proper sphere it easily becomes stiff and ponderous. And those who are not willing to follow him to the heights on which his mind and passions move will find even in his noblest writing something strained and remote. Yet perhaps for this very reason he is more precious to his little clan. After all, he never wished for a large public. 'I neither am,' he said, 'nor shall ever be popular. Such was never my ambition. But one thing is quite certain. I shall have as many readers as I desire to have in other times than ours. I shall dine late; but the dining-room will be well lighted, the guests few and select.' And he thought of his own fame no less than of the ordering of his life when he placed into the mouth of Dante these significant words: 'Let us love those that love us, and be contented to teach those that will hear us. Neither the voice nor the affections can extend beyond a contracted circle.'

1914.

V
BYRON[1]

FOR a discourse upon the caprice of human fame no
more fruitful text could be chosen than Lord Byron.
When he died at Missolonghi, little more than a century
ago, it seemed to many in England and indeed throughout Europe that the light of poetry was extinguished.
For the first time in history a contemporary English
writer was held in equal esteem at home and abroad.
Goethe proclaimed him to be the greatest genius of the
century. 'He gave', said Mazzini, 'a European rôle to
English poetry. He led the genius of England on a
pilgrimage through Europe.' It would be hard to say
whether France or Italy, Germany or Russia owed most
to his inspiration. But during the fifty years after his
death, when Byronism was giving its mood and colour
to European literature, there is little sign of his influence
upon the greater poetry of his own country, and by
English readers he was almost neglected. Through
those years we can trace in succession the slow awakening to the genius of Wordsworth, the popularity of
Tennyson, the growing admiration for Byron's contemporaries, Shelley and Keats, the cult of the Pre-
Raphaelites and of Swinburne, and lastly the tardy
recognition of Browning. The Victorian age, with all
its short-comings, was a great poetic age, a great age,
too, in the history of poetic appreciation: but with all
its varied interests it found no place for Byron; and the
years that have followed, ready as they have been to
hold up the Victorian age to scorn, have shown little
tendency to reinstate Byron upon his pedestal. The
amateur psychologist has, indeed, found in Byron's biography material of a kind that is irresistibly attractive

[1] A lecture delivered from the Chair of Poetry before the University
of Oxford, 1933.

to his taste, but the minute exploration of the more
scandalous episodes in Byron's private life has, on the
whole, tended to divert interest from his writings,
rather than to illumine and resuscitate them. 'Who
now reads Cowley?' asked Pope concerning the idol of
a previous generation. We might ask, as pertinently,
'Who now reads Byron?' Why is it that Byron, who
was devoured so passionately a century ago, is so little
read to-day?

Continental critics have found the answer in the
prudery and hypocrisy of the English people. But
though there may once have been some grain of truth
in that explanation, no one conversant with the modern
English reader, and what he reads, would credit it now.
Two other reasons—the one artistic, the other in part
intellectual, in part emotional—would seem to have
more validity.

During the past century there has been a steady
advance in the power of appreciating perfect poetic
form. Much great poetry has taken the form of lyrics.
In the ideal lyric music and meaning are one; the language and the form are alike inevitable. But Byron
with all his energy and swiftness and passion was on the
whole a careless artist; with a fine rough rhythm of his
own, but with no magical power over words, no subtlety
in verse-music. Hence, though no poet ever concentrated more fully on the expression of himself, he never
succeeded in the lyric, which is the form above all
suited for direct self-expression. A few of his lyrics
indeed find their place in every anthology—'She walks
in beauty, like the night', 'There be none of Beauty's
daughters', 'The "Isles of Greece"'. They have, doubtless, a vigour and a colour of their own, but how poor
and obvious is their music beside that of Shelley or
Keats, Tennyson or Robert Bridges! Byron sets his
emotion to a familiar, almost hackneyed, tune: the
true lyrist, even if he accept a conventional framework,

weaves upon it his own melody, of which every cadence seems responsive to the finer shades of his emotion.

Byron first made his immense reputation as a writer of romance. But his tales of love and war with their Oriental setting seem crude and rough beside the delicate beauty of Coleridge or Keats. He creates no 'atmosphere' of remoteness, and yet, what to his own day seemed intensely alive and modern is distant from us as the world of *Christabel* or *St. Agnes Eve,* but without their dreamy fascination and their deeper reverberations. Byron's romantic poetry seems clumsy and rather blatant, and it lacks that sense of style which alone could have kept it alive in a generation not its own. His romances satisfy the fastidious taste as little as his lyrics.

Nor does the modern reader find in Byron the requisite food for his intellect or his higher emotions: when he does not read poetry from sheer love of form, or to satisfy his craving for beauty, he seeks pregnant or subtle thought, or an imaginative reading of the world about him. But the ideas of Byron strike him as obvious, and he feels, and rightly, that Byron lacks what we call *vision.* He presents things as they appear to him with none of that penetrative imagination that Wordsworth had taught us to expect from the poet: he was nothing of a seer. Byron appealed chiefly to a public which, if it exists to-day, does not read poetry, reads novels— perhaps does not read at all.

But the judgement of to-day is not necessarily the right or the final one; and, perhaps, it may be worth our while to consider what Byron was to himself and to his own time; and from this he may gain a juster value even for us.

From both his parents Byron had inherited a wayward and passionate nature. For generations the Byrons had been notorious for their reckless daring and their contempt for the laws of decent society. Of his grand-uncle, the fifth Lord Byron, 'the wicked lord' as he was

known, who killed his cousins in a duel, many wild
legends were rife: they were doubtless exaggerated, but
had at least some basis in fact. His grandfather had
romantic adventures on the high seas: his father, known
as 'Mad Jack', was a heartless profligate: he ran off with
the wife of a Marquess, and after he had married her,
grossly ill-used her. His second wife, the mother of
the poet, was Miss Catherine Gordon, an heiress who
boasted descent from the Stuarts. He squandered her
fortune and then deserted her, leaving her a bare pit-
tance on which to rear their infant son. But the school
of adversity into which she had married did not teach
her any lessons as a mother. Mrs. Byron loved her child,
but had no notion of how to treat him. He was proud
and she fostered his pride. He was lame and morbidly
sensitive to it; and she taunted him with being a lame
brat. He grew up a solitary child, spoiled from infancy,
well-born, but ill-bred; intensely shy, but hiding his
shyness under an offensive swagger; affectionate, but
with none on whom to lavish his affections, and embittered through lack of responsive sympathy; of quick
temper and easily resentful, with an inherited thirst for
adventure and with a genius equal to that of any modern
youth for detecting the weakness in the armour of those
who took upon themselves to educate him.

While still a Harrow schoolboy he fell deeply in love
with his cousin Mary Chaworth, who, two years older
than himself, was already a woman. His love was not
returned; but even that thoughtless cruel remark of
hers that he overheard, 'Do you think that I could care
for that lame boy?', though it cut his sensitive nature
to the quick, did not end his passion for her, and her
marriage with a stupid fox-hunting neighbour, which
turned out as unhappily as would be expected, still
further embittered him. He felt that if he had married
her the whole course of his life would have been different, and years later, in his poem *The Dream*, he recorded

his sense of what might have been. At Cambridge he lived the life of wild dissipation common to the nobility of his time; then he travelled through Europe to the East, published, on his return, the first two cantos of *Childe Harold's Pilgrimage*, and 'awoke to find himself famous'. He became the darling of society, the shallow, corrupt, and hypocritical society of the Regency, and while he threw himself with cynical zest into all it had to offer, he had the penetration to know it for what it was. As a relief from its dull round of vapid and heartless pleasure he poured forth in rapid succession that series of Oriental romances—of love and crime and remorse—which swept readers off their feet, as no poetry has done before or since. Eastern tales were already a literary vogue: Byron was the first purveyor of them to give to his work the note of veritable experience. And many a reader found welcome escape from a timid life of monotonous labour and dreary conventional recreation, by entering into this strange new world of reckless adventure. Such readers are not over-nice in their literary tastes. And however much or little they were justified in attributing to their author an actual participation in the scenes that he described, there was no mistaking his revolt from the smug conventions of western civilization. Nor was there any doubt that in *The Giaour*, in *The Corsair*, in *Lara* he was depicting his own stormy soul. Reserved and haughty in private life, it was his habit, with a complete lack of reticence, to pour out his passion on paper. 'Poetry', he said, 'is the lava of imagination, whose eruption prevents an earthquake . . . almost all that I have written has been mere passion—passion it is true of different kinds, but always passion.' And so it was with him to the end. And after all, passion though not in itself poetry, is a necessary ingredient in it. Now, and henceforward, he made the world his confessional. Again and again, with a reiteration to us a little tedious, he drew the picture of what he was or thought himself to be. Later critics have judged him insincere. If he had felt this, they say, he could not have set it down. Yet though Byron's self-revelation had in it some element of 'pose', it was probably as near as he could get to understanding himself. From his schooldays he had the gifts of an orator, and the orator is only himself when he has an audience. Much of his writing, especially his early writing, has indeed the character of oratory as distinguished from poetry: it batters at our ears with the noise of earthquake and tempest; it does not speak to us in the still small voice heard only when the tempest has died down.

Of those fancy-dress portraits of himself that he sketched in the early Romances, this one from *Lara* has many features in common with its author:

> There was in him a vital scorn of all:
> As *if the worst had fall'n which could befall,*
> He stood a stranger in this breathing world,
> An erring spirit from another hurl'd;
>
> .   .   .   .
>
> With more capacity for love than earth
> Bestows on most of mortal mould and birth,
> His early dreams of good outstripp'd the truth,
> And troubled manhood follow'd baffled youth;
> With thought of years in phantom chase mis-spent,
> And wasted powers for better purpose lent;
> And fiery passions that had pour'd their wrath
> In hurried desolation o'er his path,
> And left the better feelings all at strife
> In wild reflection o'er his stormy life;
> But haughty still, and loth himself to blame,
> He call'd on Nature's self to share the shame,
>
> .   .   .   .
>
> Till he at last confounded good and ill,
> And half mistook for fate the acts of will:
>
> .   .   .   .
>
> So much he soar'd beyond, or sunk beneath,
> The men with whom he felt condemn'd to breathe.

But 'the worst which could befall' had not yet fallen.
Indeed the world had treated him only too well. But
it was soon to take its revenge. When his fame was at
its height came his disastrous marriage, followed a year
later by the separation from his wife, and with it a
cloud of the blackest charges against his private character—charges which may or may not have been true:
the scent is still hotly pursued by the scavengers of
literary history. The society which had idolized him
cast him off—and Byron left England never to return.
In the anguish of remorse at his own wasted life, and of
passion against the world which, despite its own vices,
had dared to pass judgement on him, he became a true
poet. His earlier writing compared with the later is little
more than facile verse. Now he rose to his full height:

> I remember [says Shelley] one remark which then
> Maddalo made. He said: 'Most wretched men
> Are cradled into poetry by wrong,
> They learn in suffering what they teach in song.'

It was the future task of Byron's genius to expose that
society which had rejected him; and, in expressing what
he knew of it, to express himself. For though it might
reject him, and he, like Milton's Abdiel, might hurl
back scorn for scorn, he could never throw off the
influence it had upon him. He was still a worldling.
This was in part his tragedy; and the plangency of
internal conflict was added to all that he was still to
write. To the execrations of outraged morality he
replied, not by defending his own actions, but by
demonstrating with fatal clearness that the only difference between him and the society which condemned
him was that *he* did not conceal his vices nor disavow
them, whilst society added to hers the meanness of
hypocrisy. He was just what this very society had
taught him to be; his life was only a reflection of hers,
the humbug cast scornfully aside. But if Byron had not
the greatness of soul to throw off this influence upon

his own character, he had at least the perception to realize what it had made of him. And the very thought of it was misery to him. Yet he was too proud to repent. As Shelley said of him: 'It is his weakness to be proud: he derives, from a comparison of his own extraordinary mind with the dwarfish intellects that surround him, an intense apprehension of the nothingness of human life. . . . His ambition preys upon itself, for want of objects which it can consider worthy of exertion.' And Sir Walter Scott described Byron as a man of real goodness of heart miserably thrown away by his contempt of public opinion. Instead of being warned or checked by public opposition, it roused him to go on in a worse strain, as if he said, 'Ay, if you don't like it, well, you shall have something worse for your pains.' Thus Byron launched, often in mere bravado, on a life of pleasure which was the wreckage of his better self, and which he knew could bring him nothing but a deeper wretchedness. Cast off by the society that had nurtured him he would carry still farther his passionate claim for the right of the individual against society. But he found that, apart from society, the individual has no life at all. And so, as Mazzini has put it, the emptiness of the life and death of solitary individuality has never been so powerfully summed up as in the pages of Byron.

> We live and die,
> But which is best, you know no more than I.

Hence it is that Byron concentrates in himself, and reflects in all his writings, the disappointed aspirations, the failure, the sorrow of his time. Others had felt this before. Shakespeare knew it, and gave it utterance in the soliloquies of Hamlet. Rousseau had expressed it in his *Confessions*. But in Byron it finds its fullest authentic voice. A sense of infinite possibilities no longer attainable, of what might have been but never can be, of remorse—vain no doubt, but far nobler than a sleek and comfortable acquiescence, weighed heavily upon Byron as they weighed heavily upon his time, and his own time recognized in him its own genius made vocal. This world-weary disillusionment is the motive that runs through that marvellous and varied stream of poetry poured forth by Byron in the years that followed his exile—the later books of *Childe Harold, The Prisoner of Chillon, The Dream, The Prophecy of Dante, Prometheus, Manfred, Cain, Don Juan.*

Childe Harold is a great rhetorical panoramic poem —torrential in its fervid eloquence—which takes us through Europe past and present; and in a series of brilliant pictures lays bare to us what is to him the one certain lesson of history. At Waterloo we tread upon 'an Empire's dust' and feel the littleness of Napoleon's ambition

> An empire thou couldst crush, command, rebuild,
> But govern not thy pettiest passion, nor,
> However deeply in men's spirits skill'd,
> Look through thine own.

Standing among the ruins of imperial Rome we read the same story:

> There is the moral of all human tales;
> 'T is but the same rehearsal of the past,
> First Freedom, and then Glory—when that fails,
> Wealth, vice, corruption,—barbarism at last.
> And History, with all her volumes vast,
> Hath but *one* page,—'t is better written here
> Where gorgeous Tyranny hath thus amass'd
> All treasures, all delights, that eye or ear,
> Heart, soul could seek, tongue ask—Away with words! draw near,

> Admire, exult, despise, laugh, weep,—for here
> There is such matter for all feeling:—Man!
> Thou pendulum betwixt a smile and tear,
> Ages and realms are crowded in this span,
> This mountain, whose obliterated plan
> The pyramid of empires pinnacled,

4989   I

Of glory's gewgaws shining in the van
Till the sun's rays with added flame were fill'd!
Where are its golden roofs? where those who dared to build?

Great men, great deeds, great cities, all have earned the
same epitaph, *vanitas vanitatum*; only nature, only
beauty endure. Upon nature therefore would he throw
himself for relief from society and from himself:

Where rose the mountains, there to him were friends;
Where roll'd the ocean, thereon was his home;
Where a blue sky, and glowing clime, extends,
He had the passion and the power to roam;
The desert, forest, cavern, breaker's foam,
Were unto him companionship; they spake
A mutual language, clearer than the tome
Of his land's tongue, which he would oft forsake
For Nature's pages glass'd by sunbeams on the lake.

Like the Chaldean, he could watch the stars,
Till he had peopled them with beings bright
As their own beams; and earth, and earth-born jars,
And human frailties, were forgotten quite:
Could he have kept his spirit to that flight
He had been happy; but this clay will sink
Its spark immortal, envying it the light
To which it mounts, as if to break the link
That keeps us from yon heaven which woos us to its brink.

Yes, even in nature the escape from self is only momen-
tary: self returns insistent and with it the sense of life
blasted, with all its disappointment and tragic failure
and betrayals—life out of tune, like sweet bells jangled:

Our life is a false nature: 't is not in
The harmony of things—this hard decree,
This uneradicable taint of sin,
This boundless upas, this all-blasting tree,
Whose root is earth, whose leaves and branches be
The skies which rain their plagues on men like dew—
Disease, death, bondage—all the woes we see,
And worse, the woes we see not—which throb through
The immedicable soul, with heart-aches ever new.

Yet let us ponder boldly—'t is a base
Abandonment of reason to resign
Our right of thought—our last and only place
Of refuge; this, at least, shall still be mine:
Though from our birth the faculty divine
Is chain'd and tortured—cabin'd, cribb'd, confined,
And bred in darkness, lest the truth should shine
Too brightly on the unprepared mind,
The beam pours in, for time and skill will couch the blind.

Our right of thought—that at least Byron will not
resign, and thought to him meant rebellion, rebellion
not merely against society, but against that religion
upon which society based its professed moral code, but
which did nothing to explain the chaos of human life.
His courage will not desert him even in his arraignment
of the Almighty. But in this struggle, as in his battle
with society, he was divided against himself. For that
knowledge of the Bible to which many a page of his
writings bears witness Byron had acquired in early
youth under orthodox teachers of Evangelical Christianity. To them every part of the Bible was equally
the revelation of the divine will and purpose. There
was no higher criticism then to distinguish the relative
authority and the moral value of the primitive myths
of Genesis, or the crude jealousies and barbaric injustice
of the tribal Hebrew God, from the nobler inspiration
of the Psalms, the prophets, or the Gospels. And Byron
was no higher critic either—he could only see the in-
adequacies of the orthodox dogmas of his day to meet
the problem of sin. How can man, he asks, be held
responsible for that sin to which he has an inherited
urge or to which he is tempted by circumstance too
strong for his nature to resist? And so he chafes against
the injustice of the orthodox doctrines of responsibility
and retribution. Byron could never, like Wordsworth,
resolve the difficulty to the satisfaction of his own soul;
yet on the other hand he could never, like Shelley,

throw it off, recapturing, free from all theological fetters, the true spirit of the religion of Christ. Shelley, indeed, averred that he could never understand the hold of orthodoxy over Byron, which, despite his reason, seemed perpetually to lie in ambush for his hours of sickness and distress. Calvinism was in his blood. 'The worst of it is that I do believe', he said. He saw no solution of the difficulty which could in any way satisfy his intellect. But at least he could rebel against it. His *Prometheus* has been called a defiant and unshakable arraignment of the conception of Providence which had been taught him by orthodox Evangelicalism. *Cain*, his most elaborate treatment of the same theme, is simply a sincere and passionate protest, a re-echo of the cry of Milton's Adam:

> Did I request thee, Maker, from my clay
> To mould me man, . . . inexplicable
> Thy justice seems.

Religious thought since Byron's time has made such strides, even among those not by nature given to obstinate questionings, that it is difficult to understand to-day either the admiration which the poem excited among a few enlightened spirits, Goethe and Shelley and Scott, or the storm of fear and horror that it aroused among the pious and orthodox, led by Bishop Heber, and reaching its ironic climax when King George IV, of blessed memory, expressed his high disapprobation of its blasphemy and licentiousness. But the storm sufficiently attests to us its power, and the part it played in the movement towards a higher truth. For in that movement rebellion against the old order was a necessary stage. Byron's attitude to religious orthodoxy, as to society, was that of a passionate rebel in conflict with something from which he could never cut himself entirely loose. He was like the half-created lion, of *Paradise Lost*, pawing to get free his hinder-parts.

But if Byron could not solve the problem of his own tormented soul, and if his own bitter experience had destroyed the idealist in him, he had all the intenser power of seeing the world about him, political and social, as it really was, and as it had been in the past. And he was a born fighter. But here, too, the foe he fought was hardly less within him than without. He has well been called 'an aristocrat in sentiment, a democrat in opinion'. As an aristocrat the past had an irresistible charm for him. He was deeply read in the history of the world and a shrewd estimator of its lessons. But while he saw the hollowness of the society from which he sprang and its incapacity for intelligent government, his proud soul loathed that Radicalism which his reason and his sense of justice called on him to embrace. He was the passionate apostle of liberty, but liberty has strange bedfellows, and the great un-washed could hardly be admitted with equanimity into the ancestral bedchamber. And so in the spirit of opposition he fought upon the side of freedom, but as a haughty foreign ally rather than as a citizen soldier, because he and the Revolutionists had a common foe, rather than because he was at one with them. Liberty has a pleasant sound to the ears of many who shudder at the thought of fraternity and equality.

The doctrines of the Revolution comprised much that was false to him. Looking back upon its whole course, he could take in its progress at a glance, and see it in its true perspective. His older contemporary, Wordsworth, lived through it, shared the ecstasy of its early promise in those days 'when to be young was very heaven', and then from its collapse suffered a tragedy so personal that he sank into a conservatism that was only a synonym for political despair. Byron could distinguish its failure in *fact*, from its spirit, which had, indeed, been defeated, but which yet survived even in defeat.

They made themselves a fearful monument!
The wreck of old opinions—things which grew,
Breathed from the birth of time: the veil they rent,
And what behind it lay, all earth shall view.
But good with ill they also overthrew,
Leaving but ruins, wherewith to rebuild
Upon the same foundation, and renew
Dungeons and thrones, which the same hour refill'd,
As heretofore, because ambition was self-will'd.

.   .   .   .

But France got drunk with blood to vomit crime,
And fatal have her Saturnalia been
To Freedom's cause, in every age and clime;
Because the deadly days which we have seen,
And vile Ambition, that built up between
Man and his hopes an adamantine wall,
And the base pageant last upon the scene,
Are grown the pretext for the eternal thrall
Which nips life's tree, and dooms man's worst—his second fall.

Yet, Freedom! yet thy banner, torn, but flying,
Streams like the thunder-storm *against* the wind;
Thy trumpet voice, though broken now and dying,
The loudest still the tempest leaves behind;
Thy tree hath lost its blossoms, and the rind,
Chopp'd by the axe, looks rough and little worth,
But the sap lasts,—and still the seed we find
Sown deep, even in the bosom of the North;
So shall a better spring less bitter fruit bring forth.

And as for the issue of this great war, that had been
crowned by the victory of Waterloo, and had over-
thrown the tyranny of Napoleon, Byron saw and re-
morselessly laid bare the truth that it had brought to
Europe not the freedom of which men spoke so idly, but
a further enslavement: *abroad*, Holy Alliances in which
Kings banded themselves together to crush out the
spirit of nationality; *at home*, a selfish and terror-stricken
reaction which paid little heed to the cries of a down-
trodden and starving people. To Wellington himself

Byron may have been unjust: his burning scorn of the
political cynicism of England under the Regency bears
the stamp not only of passionate sincerity but of fidelity
to historical fact.

Oh, Wellington! (or 'Villainton')—for Fame
   Sounds the heroic syllables both ways;
France could not even conquer your great name,
   But punn'd it down to this facetious phrase—
(Beating or beaten she will laugh the same,)
   You have obtain'd great pensions and much praise:
Glory like yours should any dare gainsay,
Humanity would rise, and thunder 'Nay!'

.   .   .   .

Though Britain owes (and pays you too) so much,
   Yet Europe doubtless owes you greatly more:
You have repair'd Legitimacy's crutch,
   A prop not quite so certain as before:
The Spanish, and the French, as well as Dutch,
   Have seen, and felt, how strongly you *restore*;
And Waterloo has made the world your debtor
(I wish your bards would sing it rather better).

You are 'the best of cut-throats:'—do not start;
   The phrase is Shakespeare's, and not misapplied:—
War's a brain-spattering, windpipe-slitting art,
   Unless her cause by right be sanctified.
If you have acted *once* a generous part,
The world, not the world's masters, will decide,
And I shall be delighted to learn who,
Save you and yours, have gain'd by Waterloo?

I am no flatterer—you've supp'd full of flattery:
   They say you like it too—'t is no great wonder.
He whose whole life has been assault and battery,
   At last may get a little tired of thunder;
And swallowing eulogy much more than satire, he
   May like being praised for every lucky blunder,
Call'd 'Saviour of the Nations'—not yet saved,
And 'Europe's Liberator'—still enslaved.

.   .   .   .

Never had mortal man such opportunity,
    Except Napoleon, or abused it more:
You might have freed fallen Europe from the unity
    Of tyrants, and been blest from shore to shore:
And *now*—what *is* your fame? Shall the Muse tune it ye?
    Now—that the rabble's first vain shouts are o'er?
Go! hear it in your famish'd country's cries!
Behold the world! and curse your victories!

What wonder that nations struggling to be free, that individuals beaten down by laws made for a class and not for a nation, saw in him their champion and viewed him as the great liberator?

But never mind;—'God save the king!' and kings!
    For if *he* don't, I doubt if *men* will longer—
I think I hear a little bird, who sings
    The people by and by will be the stronger:
The veriest jade will wince whose harness wrings
    So much into the raw as quite to wrong her
Beyond the rules of posting,—and the mob
At last fall sick of imitating Job.

Yet freedom, as Byron well knew, is not a question decided by forms of government; and democracy, now as prominent as Byron prophesied she would become, would do well to take warning from his words:

It is not that I adulate the people:
    Without *me*, there are demagogues enough,
And infidels, to pull down every steeple,
    And set up in their stead some proper stuff.
Whether they may sow scepticism to reap hell,
    As is the Christian dogma rather rough,
I do not know;—I wish men to be free
As much from mobs as kings—from you as me.

The cause of freedom was the passion of his life; and Byron fought for it with more than words. On the Italian struggle against Austria he lavished both money and energy: and when it availed nothing, he responded enthusiastically to the call of Greece. 'I am not come here', he said finely, 'in the search of adventures, but to assist the regeneration of a nation whose very debasement makes it more honourable to become their friend.' For Greece he gave his life.

My last few quotations have been taken from Byron's masterpiece *Don Juan*, the great comic epic of the modern world. Until he had written *Don Juan* with its gay prelude *Beppo*, and its tremendous off-shoot, *The Vision of Judgment*, Byron's unique and dazzling genius had not really found itself. Few poets had made more poetic and metrical experiments than he; romance, descriptive and lyrical, drama—monologue—song: in octosyllabic and heroic couplets, Spenserian stanza, blank verse—and great variety of lyrical measure. In none was he himself. Now at last he had lit upon the right form in which to present not only the many aspects of the life that he had observed, but also the many shades of his own chameleonic temperament. In other forms of poetry he has his obvious superiors. Here he shines supreme and alone. In entirely serious verse he tended, as we have seen, to oratory and declamation, and this may easily, and with him in fact did often, degenerate into rhodomontade. Such work revealed no more than one aspect of Byron, and the conception we gain from it has the falsity of a half-truth: he could only be fully and intensely himself in a poetic medium which gave him the opportunity to express at will, as he could in ordinary conversation and in his incomparable letters, the fancy of the moment, be it grave or gay, serious or burlesque, just as the mood struck him; and Byron's mood changed with the swiftness of a flash of lightning. The Italian *ottava rima*, with the traditions behind it created by Pulci, Berni, and Ariosto, was adapted alike for romance, for satire, for rapid or leisurely narrative, for comic or serious comment. But never had it been so flexible as it became in the hands of Byron. The most brilliant raconteur

since Chaucer, he poured into this mould his tales of
love and war, of shipwreck, of adventures on sea and
land, interspersed with an inexhaustible and varied
supply of relevant and irrelevant but always brilliantly
phrased digression. In this metre his musical uncertainty may add to rather than detract from the effect.
And so, the verse runs at times with the exquisite
smoothness and limpidity of a quiet stream, at times
rushes like a mountain torrent, at times saunters with
the jaunty air of a man of fashion in the Mall or Picca-
dilly, at times stumbles and lurches forward like that
same man of fashion returning home at night. Swinburne, with more elegance, has compared the stanzas
of *Don Juan* to the sea, and there is no greater authority
on either verse or the sea than Swinburne. 'They break
and glitter,' he says, 'hiss and laugh, murmur and move,
like waves that sound or subside. There is about them
a wide, wholesome air, full of vivid light, and constant
wind which is only felt at sea.' Like waves of the sea
too, we might add, hardly any successive ones are alike.
And the diction and style of which these stanzas are
composed accord, far more clearly than Wordsworth's,
with Wordsworth's own prescription of the language of
real men. Eminently simple and straightforward, with
the rarest use of poetic inversion, they run like easy
conversation, from which they rise at will to voice the
deepest emotion or to reflect the slightest nuances of
feeling. These rapid shiftings of light and shadow across
the scene of life that he presents, reflect, as no other
manner could do, his own ironic perception of the con-
tradictions in life itself, and reflect too the different
aspects which the same scene can bear when looked at
from different angles.

The main theme of the poem is life as it is lived in
the society of the governing classes of Europe and England, written by one of themselves, who knew them as
they really were. 'I take a vicious and unprincipled

character,' said Byron, 'and lead him through those ranks of society whose high external accomplishments cover and choke internal and secret vices, and I paint the natural effects of such characters. It is impossible you can believe the higher classes of society worse than they are in England, France and Italy, for no language can sufficiently paint them.' Some people have been scandalized by the picture and regarded it as merely savage satire. But Byron, let us remember, knew the society he was depicting. And so in his first twelve cantos he leads us through Spain, Greece, Turkey, Russia, and shows this heartless aristocracy at their business of diplomacy and war.

> 'Let there be light!' said God, 'and there was light!'
> 'Let there be blood!' says man, and there's a sea!

This for their business; and for the occupation of their idler hours, love—as they account love. But this, Byron tells us, is only an introduction, for in Canto XIII when Don Juan reaches England the poem is really to begin. The picture of the English country-house party, with which the poem breaks off, is as brilliant as anything that preceded it, and would be hard to excel in the pages of our realistic novelists.

> Lord Henry and his lady were the hosts;
>   The party we have touch'd on were the guests.
> Their table was a board to tempt even ghosts
>   To pass the Styx for more substantial feasts.
> I will not dwell upon ragoûts or roasts,
>   Albeit all human history attests
> That happiness for man—the hungry sinner!—
> Since Eve ate apples, much depends on dinner.
>
> .   .   .   .
>
> The gentlemen got up betimes to shoot,
>   Or hunt: the young, because they liked the sport—
> The first thing boys like after play and fruit;
>   The middle-aged, to make the day more short;

For *ennui* is a growth of English root,
  Though nameless in our language:—we retort
The fact for words, and let the French translate
That awful yawn which sleep cannot abate.

The elderly walk'd through the library,
  And tumbled books, or criticised the pictures,
Or saunter'd through the gardens piteously,
  And made upon the hot-house several strictures,
Or rode a nag which trotted not too high,
  Or on the morning papers read their lectures,
Or on the watch their longing eyes would fix,
Longing at sixty for the hour of six.

    .   .   .   .
The ladies—some rouged, some a little pale—
  Met the morn as they might. If fine, they rode,
Or walk'd; if foul, they read, or told a tale,
  Sung, or rehearsed the last dance from abroad;
Discuss'd the fashion which might next prevail,
  And settled bonnets by the newest code,
Or cramm'd twelve sheets into one little letter,
To make each correspondent a new debtor.

For some had absent lovers, all had friends.
  The earth has nothing like a she epistle,
And hardly heaven—because it never ends.
  I love the mystery of a female missal,
Which, like a creed, ne'er says all it intends,
  But full of cunning as Ulysses' whistle,
When he allured poor Dolon:—you had better
Take care what you reply to such a letter.

Much of the poem, as we all know, is not edifying
reading—a truthful picture of the private life of what
is called society could never be that, and we will admit,
at once, that Byron's is not a complete picture: but
why the reader of Fielding and of Smollett should cavil at
it is hard to understand, and assuredly it is tainted with
none of that morbidity and prurient suggestion, 'mumb-
ling at the prey it dare not bite', which is characteristic

of many a work which passes the strictest moral censor.
To the question, Why tell the tale at all? the answer is
that to be given in defence of all realistic art, which sets
out to present life as the artist sees it. Man is not an
ostrich with his head in the sand, and nothing is mended
by ignoring the truth. To the other question, Why tell
it in poetry? Byron's answer was sound enough. 'You
have so many divine poems, is it nothing to have written
a human one?' To which may be added the aesthetic
answer—that like all great works of art *Don Juan* is its
own justification. Byron could have done it in no other
way. The verse, besides giving to his subject concentration and a nicely chiselled form, lent itself aptly to
those other strains so deftly woven in with the scandalous adventures of Juan. For (as we have seen) there is
much else in the poem besides these, there is beauty,
there is romance, there is Byron's whole philosophy of
life, and above all there is the personality of Byron himself in all its shifting moods, suggesting to him an inexhaustible supply of topics which spring spontaneously
out of one another, as in that marvellous causerie with
which Book III closes, where in twenty-five stanzas he
passes, by transitions I leave you to conjecture, from
the Isles of Greece to Homer, Milton, Mrs. Milton,
Shakespeare and deer stealing, Bacon, Cromwell,
Southey and Pantisocracy and the little Bath Milliners,
Wordsworth's *Excursion* and *Waggoner*, The Ave Maria,
Dryden and Boccaccio, the soft hour of twilight, Nero,
the wooden spoon at Cambridge, and so to Aristotle's
Poetics. It would take long to do justice to the prodigal
resources and versatility of this truly marvellous poem.
Sheer poetry, without pleasantry or satire, is to be found
in the exquisite stanzas in which Byron depicts the
pathos and the beauty of young love, set in lovely
landscape of sea and sky, not spiritualized, as Shelley
would have spiritualized it, yet perhaps for all that
nearer to normal human experience.

And thus they wander'd forth, and hand in hand,
  Over the shining pebbles and the shells,
Glided along the smooth and harden'd sand;
  And in the worn and wild receptacles
Work'd by the storms, yet work'd as it were plann'd
  In hollow halls, with sparry roofs and cells,
They turn'd to rest; and, each clasp'd by an arm,
Yielded to the deep twilight's purple charm.

They look'd up to the sky, whose floating glow
  Spread like a rosy ocean, vast and bright;
They gazed upon the glittering sea below,
  Whence the broad moon rose circling into sight;
They heard the waves splash, and the wind so low,
  And saw each other's dark eyes darting light
Into each other—and, beholding this,
Their lips drew near, and clung into a kiss;

.   .   .   .

They were alone, but not alone as they
  Who shut in chambers think it loneliness;
The silent ocean, and the starlight bay,
  The twilight glow, which momently grew less,
The voiceless sands, and dropping caves, that lay
  Around them, made them to each other press,
As if there were no life beneath the sky
Save theirs, and that their life could never die.

And in these, where again there is no trace of mockery,
but simply a sense of tears for human things:

Oh, Hesperus! thou bringest all good things—
  Home to the weary, to the hungry cheer,
To the young bird the parent's brooding wings,
  The welcome stall to the o'erlabour'd steer;
Whate'er of peace about our hearthstone clings,
  Whate'er our household gods protect of dear,
Are gather'd round us by thy look of rest;
Thou bring'st the child, too, to the mother's breast.

Soft hour! which wakes the wish and melts the heart
  Of those who sail the seas, on the first day
When they from their sweet friends are torn apart;
  Or fills with love the pilgrim on his way

As the far bell of vesper makes him start,
  Seeming to weep the dying day's decay;
Is this a fancy which our reason scorns?
Ah! surely nothing dies but something mourns!

As for Byron himself, one would have to quote many stanzas to give any full conception of the many phases of himself that he presents. But the following do something to expound for us the spirit in which the poem was composed:

As boy, I thought myself a clever fellow,
  And wish'd that others held the same opinion;
They took it up when my days grew more mellow,
  And other minds acknowledged my dominion:
Now my sere fancy 'falls into the yellow
  Leaf', and Imagination droops her pinion,
And the sad truth which hovers o'er my desk
Turns what was once romantic to burlesque.

And if I laugh at any mortal thing,
  'Tis that I may not weep; and if I weep,
'Tis that our nature cannot always bring
  Itself to apathy, for we must steep
Our hearts first in the depths of Lethe's spring,
  Ere what we least wish to behold will sleep:
Thetis baptized her mortal son in Styx;
A mortal mother would on Lethe fix.

Some have accused me of a strange design
  Against the creed and morals of the land,
And trace it in this poem every line;
  I don't pretend that I quite understand
My own meaning when I would be *very* fine;
  But the fact is that I have nothing plann'd,
Unless it were to be a moment merry,
A novel word in my vocabulary.

Make as much allowance as you like for the cheap cynicism, the vulgar witticisms, the bad taste of *Don Juan*—though much of it is really better regarded as the ebullition of high spirits, of a gallantry of heart in

his sorrow—if he is indeed, as he believed, doomed to
perdition, he will at least go down with his flag flying
—there flames throughout *Don Juan* the light of a
great courageous soul, who, though he lived without
hope, never lost his courage, and fought on to the last
for a liberty that he could never gain for himself:

> And I will war, at least in words (and—should
>   My chance so happen—deeds), with all who war
> With Thought;—and of Thought's foes by far most rude,
>   Tyrants and sycophants have been and are.
> I know not who may conquer: if I could
>   Have such a prescience, it should be no bar
> To this my plain, sworn, downright detestation
> Of every despotism in every nation.

Those are proud words, but they claim no more than
the truth. To other poets we shall go to learn the full
meaning and value of the freedom that Byron sought
and never gained, to others for an interpretation of
this strange life on earth that Byron could portray but
could not fathom, to others for an idealistic vision of
what may lie beyond it: and without some such vision
there is no more to be said for it than what Byron has
said. Yet we can hardly fail to catch some inspiration
from the tremendous, remorseless power with which he
faced the facts of life as he saw them, and from the
courage of his defiance. 'Byron,' said Lord Tennyson,
'however mistaken, did yet give the world another
heart, and new pulses, and so we are kept going. Blessed
be those that grease the wheels of the old world, in so
much as to move is better than to stand still.'

VI

WALT WHITMAN[1]

IT is not difficult to explain the recent demand in this country for the writings of Walt Whitman, a demand so eager and incessant that the bookseller has often been unable to cope with it. Never before in our history has America been drawn so closely to us as now, when we have brought to happy issue a struggle in which we have fought for the same ideals and with the same invincible resolve. Those ideals, not the less universal because in the minds of many they remain vague and undefined, may, perhaps, be summed up in one word, democracy; but democracy is a word often abused and often misunderstood, and if we would get down to the elementary principles which underlie it, we shall find them nowhere more clearly and vitally expressed than in the life and work of Walt Whitman.

The full stature and significance of Whitman have not yet been widely realized in his own country. But that is not to be wondered at. For, as a critic has pertinently remarked, 'Whitman has epitomized his own people so perfectly that he could make no impression upon them. To be in America so American was obviously superfluous.' It was rather his mission to give America to the world; and it is among lovers of poetry in England, and more recently in France also, that he has come to his own. For while America has ignored or apologized for him we can see in him not only the true spirit of his own country, too often obscured for us by national prejudice, but also the inspired interpreter of that spirit which has united America with all free peoples in their struggle for freedom and justice, in their desire for a peaceable and brotherly understanding between states as between individuals, in their

---

[1] Introduction to *Selected Poems* (World's Classics, 218: first published 1920).

unshakeable belief in the right of individuals and states alike to live their own life in harmony with the rest. Whitman saw clearly enough just those problems which confront us to-day. He realized, as we do, that the intrigues of ambitious autocrats were the greatest menace to the brotherhood of the world. Thus it is interesting to recall his remark to a friend in 1888, when news reached him of the death of Frederick, Emperor of Germany: 'I am not sure of Germany now. I have no faith in this young emperor, in this William. He is a proud, narrow martinet, reactionary and dangerous, the reverse of his father in all the good things for which his father stood. Frederick would have made Germany a peace nation, but perhaps Germany was not ready for him.' Whitman had, like us, a strong hatred of the tyranny of strong nations over weak, and also, like some of us, a distrust of all barriers which one nation may erect against another in a mistaken zeal for its own prosperity. 'If America is not for freedom,' he said, 'I do not know what it is for. By God! are men always to go on clawing each other—taxing, stealing, warring —having a class to exclude and a class excluded—always to go on having favourite races, favourite castes, a few people with money here and there, and all the rest without anything everywhere?' And again, 'I am for getting all the walls down—all of them. While I love to see America prosperous I do not seem able to bring myself to desire American prosperity at the expense of other nations.' 'But must we not take care of home first of all?' he was asked. 'Perhaps, but what is home? to the humanitarian, what is home?' To him, as to Wordsworth, nationality was simply a larger form of individual human personality, and love of country was only a specialized and concentrated form of love for mankind. 'The maxims of all just law,' said Words- worth, 'and the measures of all sane practice, are only an enlarged or modified application of those dispositions of love and those principles of reason by which the welfare of individuals, in their connexion with each other, is promoted.' And, like Wordsworth, too, Whitman looked below politics to the great moral forces that lie beneath. 'The free human spirit', he said, 'has its part to perform in giving direction to history.'

These stray remarks, gleaned from the Table Talk of Whitman as an old man, are significant in their bearing upon the problems of to-day: *Leaves of Grass* records faithfully, minutely, the daring adventures of his spirit, and as we study its pages we come into close contact with a rich and stimulating personality. Whitman's inspiration is less that of an author than of a living human being. He is not primarily artist or thinker, though he is both by flashes; but few artists or thinkers have had such strange power of drawing us to themselves in a real personal attachment. He offers us his writings just as, if he were present in the flesh, he would offer us his friendship:

> Comrade, this is no book;
> Who touches this, touches a man.

Here is the secret of his spell. 'Well, he looks like a man!' Abraham Lincoln ejaculated, when he first caught sight of Whitman's splendid athletic figure striding down a street in Washington. And every page of Whitman's book is stamped with the same impression.

Walt Whitman was born at Paumanok, or Long Island, New York State, in May 1819. On both sides he came of substantial family. His father was descended from English settlers of the seventeenth century, sturdy independent farmers, who lived a hardy outdoor life; his mother had Dutch blood in her veins, though it was blended with a typical Quaker stock, with its noble traditions of simplicity, dignity, and spirituality. Whitman held firmly to the belief that he owed much to his ancestry, 'to the tenacity and central bony structure' as he calls it, 'of his English forbears', and still more to those qualities which came to him from his mother's side. 'The best of every man', he said, 'is his mother.' And the influence of his early life was both vital and permanent. As a boy he wandered at will over the long indented coast of Paumanok, in the summer bathing and racing up and down the hard sand, hunting for gulls' eggs, on little excursions with friendly fishermen, or pilots in New York Bay; in winter, when the cold was intense and the shallow creeks were frozen over, off with his comrades with hand-sledge, axe, and spear, to hunt for eels. In all seasons in the open air, riding, boating, or walking, absorbing, as he tells us, 'fields, shores, marine incidents, character, the bargemen, farmers, pilots—always had a plentiful acquaintance with fishermen—always liked the bare beach—the soothing rustle of the waves and the saline smell.' Thus he built up the magnificent physique he had inherited, and formed his tastes and character. He moved in perfect ease among the plain people. There was always something about him of the imperturbable confidence, the unsoiled freshness of nature; his face had caught the good gigantic smile of the brown old earth, and when he came to be a poet he turned for inspiration, not to his predecessors:

Oh sea [he cries], all these I'd gladly barter,
Would you the undulation of one wave, its trick to me transfer,
Or breathe one breath of yours upon my verse,
And leave its odour there.[1]

And indeed the ocean yielded to his prayer some, at

---

[1] Of his verse he said, 'Its likeness is not the stately solid palace, nor the sculpture that adorns it, nor the paintings on its walls. Its analogy is the *Ocean*. Its verses are the liquid, billowy waves, ever rising and falling, perhaps sunny and smooth, perhaps wild with storm, always moving, always alike in their nature as rolling waves, but hardly any two exactly alike in size or measure, never having the sense of something finished and fixed, always suggesting something beyond.' *With W. W. in Camden*, by H. Traubel, p. 414.

least, of her majestic secrets. It was his early training that made him what he was:

If you would understand me, go to the heights or water shore.
The nearest gnat is an explanation, and a drop or motion of
  waves a key;
The maul, the oar, the handsaw, second my words.
No shutter'd room or school can commune with me,
But roughs and little children better than they.
The young mechanic is closest to me, he knows me well,
The woodman that takes his axe and jug with him all day,
The farm-boy ploughing in the field feels good at the sound of
  my voice,
In vessels that sail my words sail, I go with fishermen and sea-
  men and love them—

The mystery, the joy, the unobtrusive greatness of Nature have more to teach him than science, or literature, or the ways of man in society. He watches, indeed, with an eager interest, the rapid developments of scientific knowledge, and pays them willing tribute, but he sees in the very positiveness of science its necessary limitations:

Your facts are useful, and yet they are not my dwelling;
I but enter by them to an area in my dwelling.

In poetry and romance he recognizes the treasure-house of the beauty and the wisdom of the past, and though never a student he is well read not only in imaginative literature but also in history and philosophy, yet

A morning glory at my window satisfies me more than all the
  metaphysics of books.
To behold the day break!
The little light fades the immense and diaphanous shadows,
The air tastes good to my palate.

And again, turning from the writings of philosopher or divine:

Logic and sermons never convince,
The damp of the night air drives deeper into my soul.

As he reflects upon the weak and petty struggles of man in society after false and enervating ideals he finds strength and example in the peaceful uncomplaining life that nature has given to the cattle of the field:

I think I could turn and live with animals, they are so placid
    and self-contain'd,
I stand and look at them long and long,
They do not sweat and whine about their condition,
They do not lie awake in the dark and weep for their sins,
They do not make me sick discussing their duty to God,
Not one is dissatisfied, not one is demented with the mania of
    owning things,
Not one kneels to another, nor to his kind that lived thousands
    of years ago,
Not one is respectable or unhappy over the whole earth.

At the age of 13 the boy was apprenticed to a printer and learned to set up type, at 17 he was acting as travelling schoolmaster in Long Island, boarding out with the families in which he taught, at 19 he had settled in New York as a bohemian of the press. Here were his headquarters for the next ten years, and he sounded all the experiences that the motley life of that strange city could offer him. He was a man of immense physical vitality, of boundless energy, filled with the joy of life. He had a passion, too, for music and the theatre, but the music that he loved best was the varied and often discordant sound of human voices in the streets, and the stage whose scenes never wearied him was the world of seething life in which the men and women about him were the players. He still found his happiest hours consorting with plain people—ferrymen and sailors, pilots and fishermen, above all with those men, now, alas, vanished from our streets, who were the epitome of all that is most breezy and most humorous in city life —'the 'bus-drivers with interrogating thumb'. 'How many hours,' he says, 'forenoons and afternoons—how many exhilarating night times I have had riding the whole length of Broadway listening to some yarn—and the most vivid yarns ever spun—and the rarest mimicry. Yes, I knew all the drivers. They had immense qualities —largely animal—but I should have trusted the general run of them in their simple good will and honour under all circumstances. Not only for comradeship and affection—great studies also I found them.' And he never let slip the opportunity of a jaunt into the neighbouring country, absorbing as before the spirit of joy from the fields, the sea, and the sky.

Then the desire of travel fell upon him—the longing to know more widely the great country to which his heart was given—and he set off through the middle states down the Ohio and Mississippi, settling for a time in New Orleans—all the time supporting himself by journalism; then again up the Mississippi, along the great lakes round by Lower Canada, and down the Hudson back to New York. Again at Brooklyn he became connected with the New York press, but he soon renounced it for the trade of carpenter and builder, doing himself much of the rougher work. The life suited him—it kept him out of doors; and freed from the hack business of a journalist he could give more thought, as he worked, to the great idea which for some time had been seething in his mind. It was his ambition to be the national poet of America, the first great prophet of modern democracy. His earlier compositions had been facile enough, but had in no way risen above mediocrity, and he knew it. But he never lacked confidence in himself. Matchless songs had been written, he said, essentially growing out of the aristocratic ideal of life and expressive of it—the development of his own land and the ideals of the future everywhere were still without their poet. He wished to put aside all earlier models and strike out a new line for himself, expressing 'his own ardours, observations, faith, and thoughts', absolutely independently; 'nothing for beauty's sake—no legend, or myth, or romance, nor euphemism, nor rhyme. But the broadest average of humanity and its identities in the now ripening Nineteenth Century, and especially in each of their countless examples and practical occupations in the United States to-day.'

In this daring break with the past Whitman followed the inevitable instinct of his own peculiar genius. For a poet can only write in the manner that is natural to him, and the true Whitman rarely finds voice save in a language and a rhythm strange to the conventions of poetry. When he adopts the recognized methods of rhyme or metre the result is not music but sing-song or a jingle; when he affects a 'poetic diction' the result is commonplace. To make this assertion is not to defend all his unconventional writing. He was, indeed, peculiarly susceptible to the dangers that beset the path of a revolutionary. He is often too conscious of his revolutionary theory, and true poetry is never written on a conscious theory. From writing simply and naturally, as the heart dictates, nothing is easier than to slip into writing on a theory of simplicity and naturalness, and the outcome is an artificiality as mannered as that of any literary school. The self-conscious man cannot express himself: a forced spontaneity is the stiffest pose. Just as Wordsworth in his duller moods relapsed into the writing of exercises that illustrate the principles in which his master-work is rooted, so Whitman, when poetic imagination flagged, poured forth a formless stream of words which is neither verse nor prose, employing a jargon as different from the picturesque and arresting colloquialism of his best poems as from that language of the plain people that he sought to represent. Many a parody of Whitman has been written; but the only parodies that have damaged his reputation are those which, unintentionally, he wrote himself. Far more than Wordsworth he lacked power to criticize himself. Conscious of his genius as an innovator, he hardened before the opposition which his innovations aroused, and in a foolish spirit of defiance became his own worst enemy. Yet in spite of that he achieved his greatest triumphs in complete freedom from the bonds of precedent. At his greatest he writes as no poet had written before him, and his style and method are justified by their success.

But if Whitman expected that the 'broad average of humanity' would recognize itself in his verse and enjoy the picture, he was doomed to disappointment. The innovator in poetry has always to create his own public, and in literature as in all else none are so conservative as the uneducated. There is no little irony in the fact that the great democracy for whom Whitman wrote saw nothing poetic in him, preferring to his strange music the most conventional ballad or hymn-tune, whilst he gained his first public among critics and poets bred in the schools that he despised. Only slowly, after more than half a century, does he gather about him that audience whom he expected to rise at his first call.

In 1855 Whitman printed the first edition of *Leaves of Grass*. Continually throughout his long life he revised, developed, and added fragments to it, but it remained in spirit and in teaching essentially the same. *Leaves of Grass* is the passionate expression of the ideal spirit of democracy as he conceived it—a call to his own people and to the world to enroll themselves as loving comrades in the struggle for freedom from all that checks the growth of the human spirit. His education among the elemental forces of nature and his association with plain and ordinary people had convinced him that the ideals of society, with its worship of wealth and rank, were utterly false.

'The melancholy prudence', he writes, 'of the abandonment of such a great being as a man is, to the toss and pallor of years of money making, with all their scorching days and icy nights,

and all their stifling deceits and underhand dodgings, or
infinitesimals of parlors, or shameless stuffing while others
starve, and all the loss of the bloom and the odor of the earth,
and of the flowers and atmosphere, and of the sea, and of the
true taste of men and women you pass or have to do with in
youth or middle age, and the insuing sickness and desperate
revolt at the close of a life without elevation or naïveté (even if
you have achieved a secure 10,000 a year and election to Con-
gress), and the ghastly chatter of a death without serenity or
majesty, is the great fraud upon modern civilization.'

For this he would substitute an ideal of simple joy and
universal comradeship. His belief in equality is absolute
and unflinching. 'As if it harmed me giving others the
same chances and rights as myself, as if it were not indispensable to my own rights that others possess the
same.'

I speak the password primeval, I give the sign of democracy,
By God! I will accept nothing which all cannot have on the
    same terms.
Whoever degrades another degrades me,
And whatsoever is said or done returns at last to me.

What he claims for man he claims also for woman.
In his perfect city 'the women walk in public proces-
sions in the streets the same as the men, they enter the
public assembly and take their places the same as the
men. It is as great to be a woman as to be a man, and
nothing is greater than to be the mother of men.' Each
is essential to the other; each is alike immortal and
divine.

And the first lesson he would teach both men and
women is their own potential greatness. They must
learn to put from them all cringing to what is outside
them, and stand erect, self-possessed, reverencing, even
glorying in the divine in their own natures. With that
religion which inculcates self-abasement Whitman will
have nothing to do. It belongs to a feudal conception
of life and must die with feudalism—the evolution of

religion must keep pace with the evolution of human society. He is himself intensely religious, but that aspect of God on which he would lay most stress is the divine man present in a measure in each of us:

I say to mankind, Be not curious about God,
For I who am curious about each am not curious about God.
Why should I wish to see God better than this day?
I see something of God each hour of the twenty-four, and each
    moment then,
In the faces of men and women I see God, and in my own face
    in the glass,
I find letters from God dropt in the street, and every one is
    sign'd by God's name,
And I leave them where they are, for I know that whereso'er
    I go,
Others will punctually come for ever and ever.

And all true worship must begin by reverencing the divine in one's self and recognizing that nothing is essentially common or unclean—that man realizes his ideal self through the noble exercise of all his functions. To Whitman soul and body are one, and the body is but the expression of the soul:

Was somebody asking to see the soul?
See, your own shape and countenance, persons, substances,
    beasts, the trees, the running rivers, the rocks and sands. . . .
Behold, the body includes and is the meaning, the main concern,
    and includes and is the soul;
Whoever you are, how superb and divine is your body, or any
    part of it!

Clear and sweet is my soul, and clear and sweet is all that is not
    my soul.
Lack one lacks both, and the unseen is proved by the seen,
Till that becomes unseen and receives proof in its turn. . . .
Welcome is every organ and attribute of me, and of any man
    hearty and clean,
Not an inch nor a particle of an inch is vile, and none shall be
    less familiar than the rest.

Such teaching was a direct challenge to orthodox opinion, and the frankness with which Whitman spoke of the body and all its uses brought upon him violent attacks from those who were honestly alarmed lest he might corrupt his fellows, as well as from others who hoped that by the expression of a pious horror they might win a cheap repute for virtue. Whitman was unmoved. He stood, through all execration, to what was to him 'the meaning of that text, "God overlooked all that he had made (including the apex of the whole— humanity with its elements, passions, and appetites) and behold, it was very good" '. In his view, the repression of all but veiled reference to the relation of the sexes— as though it were a matter to be ashamed of—was the main cause of that prurience and morbidity of mind which lies festering at the heart of the modern world. And this, he said, can only be met 'by thoughtful men and women refusing to blink the matter, but confront- ing it—assuming the essential sanity and rightness of the mysteries of birth as God ordained them, and regarding them as a central fact of humanity'. 'The subject should be redeemed', he urged, 'from the pens and tongues of blackguards and boldly brought into the demesne of poetry—as something not gross and impure, but entirely consistent with highest manhood and womanhood and indispensable to both.'

But whilst thoughtful men and women tend increas- ingly to admit the justice of his plea, Whitman has made few converts to that part of his writing in which he has striven most defiantly to drive it home. Indeed, some of his lines upon the body are no more discon- certing to the prudish than to those who are in full sympathy with his creed. The truth is that he fails less in moral than in artistic perception. The artist's busi- ness is to present his theme, whatever it be, in such a manner that it brings conviction; and as an artist he is judged by his skill in adapting means to end. It is beside the point for Whitman to urge in his own defence, 'If I had cut sex out I might just as well have left everything out.' No intelligent readers wish that he had 'cut sex out'. They wish him to have treated it with a surer poetic insight. His fault is not that he glorifies that of which he should be ashamed, but that through clumsy bungling as an artist, and a total lack of self-criticism, he cheapens and degrades that which he most desired to glorify; and that in reckless anger at that prudery which masquerades in cities under the honourable name of modesty, he allows himself to forget that true modesty is as essentially characteristic of the healthy child of nature as frankness, if, indeed, it be not its inseparable complement. Had Whitman been a finer artist he would have paid full homage to the purely physical allurements and ecstasies of sex—'the procreant urge of the world'—and yet never have obscured that spiritual meaning which was, to him, the explanation of its supremacy as natural law. In this, his central faith, he is supremely successful when he writes as a poet rather than as a defiant propagandist; and if we remove from his works the most offending passages, his true message stands out more clearly than in his full text.

A glowing love for humanity, which has its root in the physical no less surely than it transcends the physical, is the central emotion of Whitman's being, the inspiration of all he wrote. It both explains and justifies his doctrine of equality. There is no patronage in love—nothing of that condescension which is often misnamed sympathy. Love has this divine power, that he raises to his own level all that he gathers in his arms. And if we ask what it is in ourselves that Whitman calls upon us to worship, the answer surely is our authentic capacity, undeveloped as it may be, for love. As he muses upon all the fruits of civilization, ancient and modern:

Underneath Socrates I see, and underneath Christ the divine
    I see
The dear love of man for his comrade, the attraction of friend
    to friend,
Of the well-married husband and wife, of children and parents,
    of city for city, and land for land.

To those who denounce him as a revolutionary, aiming at the destruction of all existing institutions, he would reply:

What indeed have I in common with them? or what with the
    destruction of them?
Only I will establish in the Mannahatta and every city of these
    States inland and seaboard,
And in the fields and woods, and above every keel (little or large)
    that dents the water,
Without edifices or rules or trustees or any argument,
The institution of the dear love of comrades.

And for this, says Whitman, as for all the joy and the beauty of life, no man need seek in some distant El Dorado; for what is best for each of us lies in his daily path:

Will you seek afar off? you surely come back at last,
In things best known to you finding the best, or as good as the
    best,
In folks nearest to you finding the sweetest, strongest, lovingest,
Happiness, knowledge, not in another place but this place, not
    for another hour but this hour,
Man in the first you see or touch, always in friend, brother,
    nighest neighbour—woman in mother, sister, wife, . . .
You workwomen and workmen of these States having your own
    divine and strong life,
And all else giving place to men and women like you.

Here is the central part of Whitman's creed, and whatever its limitations it had at least grown out of his own vital experience: in *Calamus*, that section of his poetry which gives it direct though often mystical expression, his inner life is most intimately revealed:

Recorders ages hence,
Come, I will take you down underneath this impassive exterior,
    I will tell you what to say of me,
Publish my name and hang up my picture as that of the tender-
    est lover,
The friend the lover's portrait, of whom his friend his lover was
    fondest,
Who was not proud of his songs, but of the measureless ocean
    of love within him, and freely pour'd it forth,
Who often walk'd lonesome walks thinking of his dear friends,
    his lovers,
Who pensive away from one he lov'd often lay sleepless and
    dissatisfied at night,
Who knew too well the sick, sick dread lest the one he lov'd
    might secretly be indifferent to him,
Whose happiest days were far away through fields, in woods, on
    hills, he and another wandering hand in hand, they twain
    apart from other men,
Who often as he saunter'd the streets curv'd with his arm the
    shoulder of his friend, while the arm of his friend rested
    upon him also.

The reality of his faith soon met its supreme test. For in April 1861 the war-cloud which had for some time been gathering burst over the States, and the conflict between North and South began. It was fought primarily for the Union, though the root of dissension lay in the slave question. But as in many wars both before and since, those who had right upon their side were less well prepared for the struggle and did not prosper at the outset; and the high hopes with which they started gave way to depression and almost to despair. In the battle of Bull Run, in July 1861, the Liberation troops were routed by the more disciplined army of the South, and came pouring back to Washington in terrible disorder. But at the head of the North was one of the world's great men. Abraham Lincoln put courage into his people; and, inspiring them with his great idealism, rallied them for a continuance of the struggle. After four years' desperate fighting the Union was re-established and slavery in America was abolished.

Whitman was from the first an enthusiastic partisan of the North. He hated war, but in this contest he saw something grand and inspiring.

'We talk of our materialism,' he said, 'and it is too true. But how amid the whole sordidness—the entire devotion of America to pecuniary profit—this war for a bare idea and abstraction—a mere heroic dream, burst forth with magnificent rays, streaks of noblest heroism, fortitude, perseverance—through its malignant darkness the great National Will below and behind comprehending all and not once really wavering, what could be grander?'

He had unbounded admiration for Lincoln. His belief in the essential divinity of all men did not preclude him from hero-worship. When he spoke of equality he was not under the delusion, fatal to democracy as to any form of government, that one man is as good as another. Democracy means equality of opportunity, that from the mass may emerge those men who personify its own best spirit, who have at once the insight and the courage to translate its own highest aspiration into action, befitting the time. A true democracy breeds heroes from its own ranks and follows them in faith and loyalty, worshipping the hero, not as a thing apart, but rather as the expression of its own best self. It is no wonder, then, that Lincoln's assassination in the hour of triumph struck Whitman with a grief as profound as it was lasting. He devoted to *Memories of Lincoln* a section of the *Leaves of Grass*, and *When lilacs last in the door-yard bloomed* is assuredly among the most poignantly beautiful of the world's death-songs; and all through his life, on each anniversary of the murder, Whitman delivered a public oration recalling to the people the personality and example of this hero.

The part that Whitman himself played in the War of Liberation was humbler than Lincoln's, but no less heroic. To each man Nature assigns his fitting task: Whitman, throughout the conflict and for years afterwards, devoted himself to the care of the wounded and the dying, first on the battlefields, and then at the immense hospital barracks at Washington.

'It is only', writes a friend, 'in the light of his work at this time that his life and writings can be really understood—here his whole character culminates. To more than a hundred thousand suffering soldiers he was personally the cheering visitor, and ministered in some form or other to their direct needs of body and spirit—soldiers from every quarter, for strong as were his sympathies with the North he treated the rebel the same as the rest.'

Of his manner of life during these terrible years there is a faithful record in his letters to his mother, and in his diaries, from which, afterwards, he published *Specimen Days*; in *Drum Taps* the essence of his experience is distilled by his imagination into song. No poet had ever a finer opportunity for learning to know the heart of the soldier: none has turned his knowledge to nobler account. As he passed among the wounded and the dying he took with him the spirit of health, of love, of divine comradeship. His plan of action throughout is intensely significant and strangely characteristic of the man. Before entering upon his daily rounds he prepared himself as though for a festival. After a good rest, a bath, a complete change of clothing, he put a flower in his buttonhole and carried bunches of flowers in his hands. Over his shoulder he slung a huge haversack bulging with little gifts for the sick, which could also be seen sticking out of his pockets; when possible he would bring baskets of fruit, tobacco, lemonade, ice-cream, little presents of money—trifles all of them, but such as would cheer the sufferer—if not in themselves, for the sake of the love that brought them. 'His magnetism', we are told, 'was incredible and exhaustless. It was a fact deeper than speech. The lustreless eye brightened at his approach: his commonplace words invigorated. A bracing air seemed to fill the ward and neutralize the bad smells.' Somctimes he would read to the inmates, sometimes merely sit by the bedside and hold the hand of a dying man. Often he would write letters for them to mothers, sisters, or wives—many a love-letter he wrote, and words of comfort and of courage to bereaved relatives. Here is a typical passage from *Specimen Days*, illustrating how, for many hours a day through several years, Whitman passed his time:

'This afternoon I spent a long time with Oscar Wilber, low with chronic diarrhoea and a bad wound also. He asked me to read him a chapter of the New Testament. I opened at the close of one of the Evangelists and read the chapters describing the latter hours of Christ and the scene at the crucifixion. The poor wasted young man asked me to read how Christ rose again. I read slowly, for Oscar was very feeble. It pleased him very much, yet the tears were in his eyes. He asked me if I enjoyed religion. I said, "Perhaps not, my dear, in the way you mean, and yet maybe it is the same thing." He said, "It is my chief reliance." He talked of death and said he did not fear it. I said "Why, Oscar, don't you think that you will get well?" He said, "I may, but it is not probable." His wound was very bad; it discharged much. The diarrhoea had prostrated him, and I felt that even then he was dying. He behaved very manly and affectionate. The kiss I gave him as I was leaving he returned fourfold.'

The spirit which breathes through these simple jottings in Whitman's diary finds perfect lyrical expression in *Drum Taps*:

A sight in camp in the daybreak grey and dim,
As from my tent I emerge so early sleepless,
As slow I walk in the cool fresh air the path near by the hospital
    tent,
Three forms I see on stretchers lying, brought out there un-
    tended lying,
Over each the blanket spread, ample brownish woollen blanket,
Grey and heavy blanket, folding, covering all.

Curious I halt and silent stand,
Then with light fingers I from the face of the nearest the first
    just lift the blanket;
Who are you elderly man so gaunt and grim, with well-grey'd
    hair, and flesh all sunken about the eyes?
Who are you my dear comrade?
Then to the second I step—and who are you my child and
    darling?
Who are you sweet boy with cheeks yet blooming?
Then to the third—a face nor child nor old, very calm, as of
    beautiful yellow-white ivory;
Young man I think I know you—I think this face is the face of
    the Christ himself,
Dead and divine and brother of all, and here again he lies.

Few men have lived more fully in the spirit of their
creed than Whitman in those strenuous years of un-
remitting service. His generous spirit had nothing half-
hearted about it:

> Behold, I do not give lectures or a little charity,
> When I give, I give myself.

But this gift from a man passionately eager as he for all
the joy that life could offer was not without its heavy
price. No gift worth the having is without its cost,
and those who imagine that love, the greatest of all
gifts, entails no sacrifice—is not, indeed, the supreme
sacrifice—little know its real nature. 'They all died
about us there,' he writes, 'just about in the same way
—noble, sturdy loyal boys. I always kept an outward
calm amongst them—I had to. I would have been
useless if I hadn't. But no one could tell what I felt
underneath it all.' Once during the war his health gave
way, but he was soon back at his post; then, a year or
two after all was over and the last hospital was closed,
he was struck down with paralysis; and though after
some years' complete retirement he rallied and lived to
be an old man, he never regained his former health.
He gave his life for his country as truly as if he had

fallen upon the field of battle. His belief in the duty, the necessity, of joy in life, was again put to a sore trial. But he realized that joy had its full significance for those only who had passed through the valley of the shadow. He remembered how, a child, wandering on the sea-shore, he had witnessed one of nature's remorseless tragedies. Day by day he had watched two sea-birds:

Two feather'd guests from Alabama, two together,
And their nest, and four light-green eggs spotted with brown,
And every day the he-bird to and fro near at hand,
And every day the she-bird crouch'd on her nest, silent with
  bright eyes,

and deep into his soul had sunk the agonizing screams of the desolate he-bird, bereft by some cruel chance of his mate. In manhood he proved this upon his own heart, and out of the memory of childhood had woven one of his most intimate and beautiful songs, 'Never more the cries of unsatisfied love be absent from me'. And now that he had passed through the torturing experience of the war his vital energy was sagging low, and for all his cheery manner he lived much in the never-to-be-forgotten past; so that 'many a face of anguish', and 'the dead on their backs with arms extended wide' would haunt his dreams in sleep. He was sick, and often lonely, conscious that his message was ignored by the bulk of his people, and that others who heard it branded him as a wilful and licentious perverter of public morals. It was in such a mood that he expressed himself in the prayer of the dying Columbus, in his lifetime dis-credited and deserted, yet having before him at his death a vision of the future of that great country he had discovered:

And these things I see suddenly, what mean they?
As if some miracle, some hand divine unseal'd my eyes,
Shadowy vast shapes smile through the air and sky,
And on the distant waves sail countless ships,
And anthems in new tongues I hear saluting me.

Thus in his uttermost distress Whitman retains his power of hope; in his belief in what the future may bring forth he is optimist to the last. But his optimism does not spring from ignorance, or indifference to the dark forces that combat it. He is not blind or callous to the sin and sorrow of the world:

I sit and look out upon all the sorrows of the world, and upon
    all oppression and shame,
I hear secret convulsive sobs from young men at anguish with
    themselves, remorseful after deeds done,
I see the wife misused by her husband, I see the treacherous
    seducer of young women,
I mark the ranklings of jealousy and unrequited love attempted
    to be hid, I see these sights on the earth,
I observe the slights and degradations cast by arrogant persons
    upon labourers, the poor, and upon negroes, and the like;
All these—all the meanness and agony without end I sitting
    look out upon,
See, hear, and am silent.

He could see and hear all this, and accept it without flinching, though it ate into his soul, because he felt it to be transitory, and the spirit of man immortal, because he believed intensely in life and in the destiny of all human beings. And so he set himself resolutely to interpret the good that lies hidden beneath the surface of evil. In a poem entitled *Faces* he refuses to be deluded by the mean and haggard disguises under which men conceal their infinite possibilities—the cheat, the murderer, the idiot—in the faith that sooner or later the true man will emerge; and *To a Common Prostitute*, at whom the Pharisee is ever ready to cast a stone, he speaks in language which for all its homely phrasing re-echoes the words of Christ to Mary Magdalene or the woman of Samaria.

'I myself', he said, 'see clearly enough the crude streaks in the strata of the common people, the vast collections of the ignorant, the credulous, the unfit, the incapable, the very low and poor. But the chief aim of all government is to develop, to open up to cultivation, to encourage the possibilities of that aspiration for independence and pride and self-respect latent in all character.' He had evidence enough, as we have, of the root qualities of the people when they are inspired by noble ideals, and led by worthy leaders. 'Grand, common stock,' he writes, 'convincing growth, prophetic of the future—proof undeniable of perfect beauty, tenderness, and pluck that never feudal lord, nor Greek nor Roman yet rivalled. Let no tongue speak their disparagement to one who has been through the war in the great army hospitals.' But he realized the need of development. Both for the race and for each individual there must be a future to correct and to complete the past. Thus he could only view our failures in the light shed upon them by immortality, and with this unswerving faith he never despaired. He always felt at ease about death, and as he grew older its 'heavenly whispers' brought ever more grateful music to his ears, 'Do you think life so well provided for, and Death, the purport of all Life, is not provided for?' he asks. During the war he must have seen thousands die—but death was not among the horrors of war—it was the end of them. It banished hatred and brought to the dead peace, and to the living reconciliation:

Reconciliation, word over all, beautiful as the sky,
Beautiful that war and all its deeds of carnage must in time be
    utterly lost,
That the hands of the sisters Death and Night incessantly softly
    wash again, and ever again, this soil'd world;
For my enemy is dead, a man divine as myself is dead,
I look where he lies white-faced and still in the coffin—I draw
    near,
Bend down and touch lightly with my lips the white face in the
    coffin.

Death is indeed a mystery, but life is a mystery

also. To meet death well assuredly needs courage; but no more courage than manfully to face life; and if there is sorrow it is not with the dead but with those who remain behind.

With this faith in human destiny Whitman summons us to his side. Many of his poems are trumpet calls that every man who would not remain dungeoned in conventions, and bound by outward formulas, should follow him on the open road of self-reliance that leads to the city of freedom:

A great city is that which has the greatest men and women,
If it be a few ragged huts it is still the greatest city in the whole
world.

It is for us to seek it, or to make it, at our doors. But his own experience forbids him to delude us into thinking of his gospel of joy and love and freedom as one easy either to accept or to fulfil. It is a life of conflict beset with difficulties and dangers, oppressed with misunderstandings, calumnies, denunciations. Such is always the struggle for emancipation, whether the emancipation sought be national or political, or that without which political freedom is worse than useless, the emancipation of the mind. Yet the man who is fully possessed with reverence for himself and love for his fellows will not hesitate. What though defeat is as likely as victory?

Hurrah! for the conquered,
Battles are lost in the same spirit as they are won.

Whatever our own lot we may rest assured that in the end victory will go with the pioneers, even if they do not live to reap the fruits of it themselves. For them it is enough that they are on the right side, fighting in the spirit of loving comradeship for the development of a spiritual and heroic democracy:

Not for delectations sweet,
Not the cushion and the slipper, not the peaceful and the studious,
Not the riches safe and palling, not for us the tame enjoyment,
Pioneers! O pioneers!

> Do the feasters gluttonous feast?
> Do the corpulent sleepers sleep? have they lock'd and bolted
>> doors?
> Still be ours the diet hard, and the blanket on the ground,
>> Pioneers! O pioneers!

> Has the night descended?
> Was the road of late so toilsome? did we stop discouraged
>> nodding on our way?
> Yet a passing hour I yield you in your tracks to pause oblivious,
>> Pioneers! O pioneers!

> Till with sound of trumpet,
> Far, far off the daybreak call—hark! how loud and clear I hear
>> it wind,
> Swift! to the head of the army!—swift! spring to your places,
>> Pioneers! O pioneers!

That 'daybreak call' is sounding in our ears to-day, and if we pay no heed to it the night that follows can have no end. If the world is to survive the wreck of these last cruel years and not bring upon itself a wreck more deadly still, it can only be through the application to life of such principles as a study of Whitman suggests. Without it no peace, however just, can be lasting.

> Were you looking to be held together by lawyers?
> Or by an agreement on a paper? or by arms?
> Nay, nor the world, nor any living thing, will so cohere.

Many look to a League of Nations to solve some of our acutest problems. Yet, as Lord Grey has wisely said, a League of Nations is but machinery, and machinery is useless unless it has behind it those willing and able to work it. It must be backed by the active and potent will of the peoples, ready even at some sacrifice to give it their support. And assuredly we may hope that from this welter of blood and tears the world has learnt its lesson:

Over the carnage rose prophetic a voice,
Be not dishearten'd, affection shall solve the problems of freedom yet,

Those who love each other shall become invincible . . .
Sons of the Mother of All, you shall yet be victorious,
You shall yet laugh to scorn the attacks of all the remainder of
    the earth.

For Liberty, Equality, Democracy, what are these to
Whitman but the spirit of divine comradeship?

These shall tie you and band you stronger than hoops of iron,
I, ecstatic, O partners! O lands! with the love of lovers tie you.

1919.

VII

THE INTERPLAY OF LITERATURE AND SCIENCE DURING THE LAST THREE CENTURIES[1]

IN his series of Addresses on 'Science and Education', Thomas Huxley spoke as the foremost champion of scientific studies at a time when those studies were still inadequately endowed, and had to fight for recognition against vested interests and conservative obscurantism; and it was his main thesis that,

'apart from all questions of its practical importance, a knowledge of science, its principles and results, which have so profoundly modified society and have created our modern civilisation, will give a culture unattainable by any form of education which neglects it.'

But in maintaining this thesis he showed himself to be no enemy to the arts. 'I am the last person', he said, 'to question the value of a genuine literary education, or to suppose that intellectual culture can be complete without it.' He recognized the intrinsic value of classical learning, even while he insisted that the student of science had no time to spare for it: the culture necessary for *him*, he argued, must be gained from his own literature; and to the value of English literature Huxley paid a tribute that should satisfy its most devoted adherent. On re-reading his discourse, one feels that if he were alive to-day, his chief regret would be that the urgency of specialism leaves scant leisure for the humaner studies. For 'an exclusively scientific training', he said, 'will bring about a mental twist as surely as will an exclusively literary training'.

In maintaining this point of view Huxley was no exception among scientists. His contemporary Tyndall

[1] Huxley Lecture delivered in the University of Birmingham, 1938. Reprinted from the *Hibbert Journal*, vol. xxxvii.

tells how he was spurred on in the pursuit of science by inspiration drawn from Tennyson; Darwin records his intense delight as a youth in Shakespeare and Milton, Wordsworth and Shelley; and when in later years he lost his taste for poetry he was profoundly conscious that his life was maimed and stunted; Humphry Davy and Rowan Hamilton of quaternion fame, were addicted throughout their lives to the writing of verse. It was not, I admit, of a very high quality; I have perused much of it, if not with the 'dreadful indifference' with which Jane Austen's hero read the tender lines of Cowper, at least with his 'impenetrable calm'. But its lack of merit is not surprising. Literature is a vocation and not a pastime, and supreme success in it depends not only on a special bent of genius, but also on application as strenuous as science demands of her votaries. The significant fact is that they felt constantly impelled to write it. And men of science have at times been genuine poets. Such in the second century was Ptolemy the astronomer:

> Mortal tho' I be, yea ephemeral, if but a moment
> I gaze up to the night's starry domain of heaven,
> Then no longer on earth I stand; I touch the Creator,
> And my lively spirit drinketh immortality.

And so in our times Sir Ronald Ross, in verse which has never won its due meed of recognition, set down his spiritual diary of seven long years of exile devoted to researches into tropical malaria. But whatever his literary gifts or taste, the scientist, like the rest of us, inhabits a world of thought and feeling and action wherein science plays but a subordinate part, and of that world literature is the written record.

For whereas the business of science is to ascertain, and to set in intelligible and ordered relation, the facts of the physical world, literature takes as her province the life of man in all its aspects, and working through the feelings quickens that life to a higher consciousness.

Of man as a social being science has little to tell us, of his life as an individual nothing. It may indeed convince his reason that in this vast universe he is but an atom wholly without significance, yet he remains the centre of his own world—a world greater than that of which science is cognizant, seeing that without it science itself would have no meaning. 'Man', as the poet assures us, 'is a spiritual being, and the proper work of his mind is to interpret the world according to his higher nature, and to conquer the material aspects of the world so as to bring them into subjection to the spirit.'

But the material aspects of the world must be recognized if they are to be conquered; and when prevalent notions of the universe, of man's origin and destiny, are revolutionized, or modified, or even challenged by science, literature cannot ignore it; whilst the effects of scientific discovery on social conditions are inevitably reflected in the mirror of literary art.

That eager interpretation of nature which had slept since the great days of Athens reawakened in the Italy of the fifteenth century, and gradually spread through Europe. In thought it implied an escape from the trammels of scholastic authority; in the arts a closer study and a keener delight in the human form, and a fearless delineation of the character and passions of man; in science a sense of the illimitable possibilities of knowledge, if slavish acquiescence in tradition were replaced by exact observation and careful experiment. Heralded by Copernicus in astronomy, and Vesalius in anatomy, the new movement slowly gathered force, and its flood-tide swept our shores in the seventeenth century, the first great age of modern science. Gilbert's book on magnetism had appeared in 1599: there followed, to name only a few outstanding achievements, Napier's work on logarithms, Harvey's discovery of the circulation of the blood, Boyle's researches in chemistry and physics; the climax was reached by the supreme and comprehensive genius of Isaac Newton, whose *Principia* appeared in 1687.

The prophet of the movement was a great man of letters, Francis Bacon. Modern critics have belittled his importance in the history of science, asserting that he had no insight into its true principles and method: even in his own day Harvey complained that Bacon wrote philosophy like a Lord Chancellor. But such is human nature, that a Lord Chancellor, and one moreover gifted with an incomparable power over language, may catch the ear and the imagination of a people who would be deaf to the more halting accents of an obscure researcher. Science was at least the master passion of Bacon's life; he saw within man's grasp a vast unexplored kingdom of knowledge, 'if only he will be humble enough and patient enough and truthful enough to occupy it', and he constituted himself its champion. It was largely due to his eloquence that matters which had otherwise been the concern of specialists became the common interest of educated men. Bacon, in fact, created for science an intellectual atmosphere in which it might live and thrive. His immediate successors are the best judges of his influence: to them he was the Moses of science, and if, like Moses, he never entered Canaan, he yet—

> Did on the very borders stand
> Of the blest promised land,
> And from the mountain top of his exalted wit
> Saw it himself and showed us it.

The widespread interest which Bacon did so much to foster was not slow to affect imaginative literature. Superficially it is evident in the frequent metaphors and analogies which the poets draw from the processes or instruments of science, replacing allusions to classical story, or to common natural phenomena, by references to compasses and perspective glasses, to pulleys and the magnet. Davenant, indeed, with conscious pride, admits that he 'is obliged for his imagery to men of science, as well mechanical as liberal'; and so general was this obligation that a century later, when literary taste had altered, Dr. Johnson notes it as a merit in Waller that he 'seldom fetches an amorous sentiment from the depths of science'. But this was only a ripple on the surface. Of the manner in which science was soon to deflect the whole current of thought, the two greatest poets of the age, Donne and Milton, alone had any real presentiment.

> The new philosophy calls all in doubt,
> The element of fire is quite put out;
> The sun is lost, and the Earth, and no man's wit
> Can well direct him where to look for it.

So wrote Donne when the movement was still in its infancy, and the Copernican theory as yet mathematically unproven. As a matter of fact, the new philosophy was soon to achieve just what Donne denied it. For it directed man's wit where truly to place the sun, discrediting the time-honoured concentric scheme of the universe. But despite his eager, restless mind, Donne was a disciple of the old scholasticism, and the new science impressed him less as an intellectual triumph than with the uncertainty of all human knowledge. Apprehensive of an imminent clash of science with theology, he does not attempt to resolve the dissonance, but falls back on the transcendence of the spiritual and the vanity of earthly life. And his significance lies not in this conclusion, which may seem lame and impotent, but in the sceptical undercurrent which troubles his religious consciousness, as the religious consciousness was not again to be troubled until well into the nineteenth century.

Milton's attitude was different. He had visited the 'famous Galileo, grown old, a prisoner to the Inquisition for thinking in astronomy otherwise than the Franciscan and Dominican licensers thought', and while he adopted for the imaginative setting of his epic the traditional Ptolemaic system, there is evidence in plenty that he was abreast of informed astronomical theory. But though his conception of 'a complete and generous education' included a practical knowledge of the sciences, he foresaw, with his aristocratic contempt for the intelligence of the 'miscellaneous rabble', the dangers of a little knowledge, imperfectly comprehended. 'Adam', we read, 'inquires concerning celestial motions, is doubtfully answered, and exhorted to search rather things more worthy of knowledge.' Yet if Milton seems here to disparage astronomical science, it should be borne in mind that in *Paradise Regained* he denounces, with even greater force, his own favourite studies. The Hebraic and Hellenic strains within him were ever at war. And so, whilst his Hebraism discouraged all secular learning, his Hellenism inspired a very different mood. 'Give me the liberty to know, to utter and to argue, according to conscience, above all liberties.' In that passionate outcry Milton laid down the conditions under which alone knowledge can prosper.

The scientific movement, retarded for a time by the Civil Wars, gained its central laboratory and, as it were, its temple in the Royal Society, which grew out of informal meetings, held in Oxford and London, of a small group of scientists, and received its charter in 1662. Here its aims were formulated and its methods of procedure laid down—'to improve and enlarge the empire of operative philosophy by the real effects of the experimental'. In conception the Society owed not a little to the suggestions of literature, to Solomon's House in Bacon's *New Atlantis*, to Cowley's *Propositions for the Advancement of Experimental Philosophy*; and among its original members were most of the acknowledged leaders of the literary world—Denham, Evelyn, Waller, Cowley, and Dryden. Their eulogies gave it the prestige which Bacon had brought to the earlier stages of the movement. Thus Dryden introduced into his *Annus Mirabilis* a prophecy of its future greatness, and contrasted his own independent approach to literature with the current subservience to authority in the words: 'I must take leave to say that my whole discourse is sceptical, according to the way of reasoning initiated in the modest inquisitions of the Royal Society.' But Cowley, of all poets then most widely esteemed, was its self-appointed laureate. His verses to his *Mistress* are cold and uninspired: they might, as Johnson drily remarks, have been 'written for penance by a hermit, or for hire by a philosophical rhymer who had only heard of another sex'. But when he hymns the heroes of science, and glorifies the great principle—*not words but things*—to which they owed their triumphs, a touch of genuine poetic fire descends upon him. In his Odes *on Mr. Harvey, on Mr. Hobs,* and *to the Royal Society* Cowley is at his best.

But he, no more than his fellows, realized the metaphysical issues involved in the movement that he extolled. When Hobbes, who 'passed as a mathematical man, though', says Burnet rather unkindly, 'he knew little that way,'—expounded in his *Leviathan* a philosophy based on the materialistic principles of the new science, Cowley hesitated to vouch for its eternal truth: ' 'Tis only God', he says with commendable modesty,

> 'Tis only God can know
> Whether the fair idea thou dost show
> Agrees *entirely* with his own, or no.

Yet despite this uncertainty as to the Deity's views on materialism, there can be no doubt of its pervading influence; and no doubt, either, that the intimate association in the Royal Society of men of letters with men of science did much to accelerate the change that was coming over literature, and through literature over contemporary thought. That change has been defined as a shifting of values from the next world to this. The great writers of the early seventeenth century were preoccupied with problems of man's ultimate destiny, with the struggles and aspirations of the individual soul. But attention was now focused upon the actual world in which we live; men were brought down from heaven to earth; the effects of scientific discovery upon many sides of their social life could not fail to fascinate them, and something of the principles that inspired it filtered into their minds. Their child-like faith in tradition was ousted by common sense, and the darker forms of superstition fell into disrepute. Thus Hutchinson, in his *History of Witchcraft* (1718) directly attributes the decline in the persecution of witches to the spread of the new learning, and pays eloquent tribute to the Royal Society as 'one of the noblest foundations in Europe, and very salutary to this country'. But it was an age of transition, wherein many men of high intelligence still lived in the old world as well as in the new. Hutchinson goes on to tell how, at a memorable trial in 1664, the famous physician and man of letters, Sir Thomas Browne, helped to convict two wretched women, by stating that he was 'clearly of opinion that their fits were natural, but heightened by the devil, co-operating with the malice of the witches', and he added that 'in Denmark there had lately been a great discovery of witches, who used the very same way of afflicting persons, by conveying pins into them'. 'Sir Thomas', comments Hutchinson with a just scorn, 'decided the case, not with the addition of any argument, but on the authority of some books from Denmark.' Thus Browne, for all his forward-looking devotion to scientific experiment, and his genuine desire to explode *Vulgar Errors*, could not give up his faith in the devil, that last infirmity of the religious

4989 M

mind. The Royal Society stood for principles which Browne too professed, though he could not always be faithful to them. It insisted on a rational view of the world, and its influence gradually permeated both literature and society.

It affected the style of literature no less than its general temper and subject matter. The gorgeous eloquence, the profuse imagery, the elaborate but often contorted sentence-structure of our earlier prose was little suited to present needs: the Royal Society, we are told, 'exacted from all its members a close natural way of speaking, positive expressions, clear senses, a native easiness, bringing all things as near the mathematical plainness as they can'. The revolution in style, here advocated in the interests of science, was successfully achieved because contemporary men of letters were as fully convinced of its necessity. To literature there resulted a loss in beauty of rhythm, in colour, in the power of mysterious suggestion, but also indubitable gain. Prose now became an adequate instrument of clear thinking and common sense, a fitting vehicle for history and biography, for essay and novel; and science gained models from which to learn that difficult but indispensable art of lucid and logical expression.

Thus while science in the seventeenth century gave literature a new orientation, it owed to literature not only its prestige, but also the perfection of an instrument essential to its progress. Literature performed a service hardly less useful when it held up to ridicule the errors and extravagances incident to the childhood of the movement. Fired with a zeal for discovery, its votaries could not always distinguish fruitful investigation from idle curiosity. This is evident to anyone who glances at some of the entries in the early pages of the Society's *Transactions*:[1] 'The Duke of Buckingham

---

[1] *v.* 'English Letters and the Royal Society in the Seventeenth Century', by F. P. Wilson, *Mathematical Gazette*, December 1935. I owe

promised to bring to the Society a piece of an unicorn's horn. . . .' 'Mr. Long affirmed that he could show a pebble that doubled its size in a short time. . . .' 'The amanuensis produced artificial serpents, which, being fired, and cast into the water, burnt till they bounced. . . .' 'Sir John Finch's piece of an incombustible hatband was produced', and so on. Moreover, for the only time, perhaps, in its history, science was now a fashionable craze. With a king who graced the dissecting table with his presence, and was a keen chemist, what more natural than that aspirants to the *haut ton* should affect the same tastes? Membership of the Royal Society was not so exclusive as to-day; it admitted many virtuosi, as they were called—ignorant amateurs, whose easy gullibility and vain pretensions to learning brought the whole Society into disrepute. To the satirists they fell an easy prey. Samuel Butler, prince of lampoonists, depicts a meeting at which the members, directing their telescope to the heavens, observe a battle raging in the moon and a monstrous elephant dealing dire destruction among the combatants. Forthwith they proceed to enter in the *Transactions* this astronomical portent, only to learn, on dismantling their telescope, that the men-at-arms were flies on the glass, and that the elephant was 'a mouse that, by mishap, Had caught himself, and them, in the optic trap'.

Similarly, the dramatist Shadwell presents a man of fashion who has spent £2,000 on a microscope to study the mites in his cheese, but is grossly ignorant of human nature. ' 'Tis below a virtuoso', he says, 'to trouble himself with men and manners. *I* study insects.' And in the next generation, when literature, intent on social life, had ceased to take a serious interest in science, the ridicule persisted, arguing a real insensibility to the value of that movement which their predecessors had

this reference, and also the quotation from Shadwell, *infra*, to Professor Wilson's valuable paper.

so eagerly welcomed. In Pope's *Dunciad*, among the first to receive a degree from the Goddess of Dulness are those who 'Shine in the dignity of F.R.S.' Swift's satire is even more scathing. When Gulliver visits the College of Lagado, he meets one professor who has striven for eight years to extract sunbeams from cucumbers, and another devising a plan for building a house from the roof downwards. And the wonders achieved by the newly perfected microscope only afford Swift a witty analogy with the minor poet who rails at his superiors:

> So Naturalists observe a flea
> Hath smaller fleas that on him prey;
> And these have smaller fleas to bite 'em
> And so proceed *ad infinitum.*

Addison alone, among leading men of letters in the early eighteenth century, had any real appreciation of science. 'No writers', he affirms in the *Spectator*, 'more gratify and enlarge the imagination than the authors of the new philosophy, whether we consider their theories of the earth or heavens, the discoveries they have made by glasses, or any other of their contemplations of nature.' 'Science', he concludes, 'opens infinite space on every side of us, but the imagination is at a stand.'

In Addison's just comment on the thought of his age there is unconscious irony. For the contraction which he deplores was itself largely due to the influence of the scientific movement, and those writers who now mocked at science were themselves the victims of the narrow rationalism which it had inaugurated. They shared its limitations without doing justice to its achievement. The mechanistic outlook on the universe had in truth invaded all spheres of thought. Nowhere is this more evident than in the sphere of religion. The early scientists, intent as they were on their own problems, were yet for the most part men of unimpeachable orthodoxy, and eager to prove their researches to be compatible with religious faith: the writers of the eighteenth century, though not themselves scientists, were largely occupied in arguing whether revealed religion were compatible with the findings of science, with proving or disproving the *reasonableness* of Christianity; and whatever conclusion they reached, the essential spirit of religion evaporated in the process. Of this Pope's *Essay* which 'vindicates the ways of God to man' is an obvious example. Richard Bentley, the great classical scholar, and the one notable man of letters who took a serious interest in science, applied to Newton for proofs of Christianity with which to rout the Deists, and in Newton's reply, that 'the planetary system argues a first cause not blind and fortuitous, but very well skilled in mechanics and geometry', religion was held to have scored a signal victory. Yet it is not when he is solving mathematical problems that a man feels most need of a God; and in the literature of the age there was little to satisfy the cravings of the soul. The philosophy which Mr. Spectator 'brought from schools and colleges to dwell in clubs and assemblies, at tea tables and in coffee houses', had nothing transcendental about it; it was rational, utilitarian; in this, characteristic of the whole epoch. Its essential spirit is summed up in the words of Dr. Johnson, its greatest personality, 'The noblest beauties of art are those of which the effect is co-extended with *rational* nature, or at least with the whole circle of polished life.'

It was the conviction that this point of view left out, and by implication seemed to repudiate, the better part of man, that occasioned the great literary revival with which the century closed. In philosophy, indeed, the reaction had come earlier with Berkeley; but Berkeley's idealism had fallen on deaf ears. In literature it took the form of a return to nature—to *real* nature as opposed to the *rational* nature applauded by Dr. Johnson. Of this revival Wordsworth was the prophet and the inspiring genius; and his views have a special importance, as they constitute the first attempt in our imaginative literature seriously to face the problem of the relation of scientific thought to the spiritual life. The mind of man was the main region of Wordsworth's song, and in the mind of man, as he knew it within himself, he found elements that the mechanistic conception of nature was wholly incompetent to explain. From youth up he had been haunted by mysterious presences in the sky and in the hills, and his experience convinced him of the reality of a vast world which can only be comprehended by a quality which he terms imagination, a quality not irrational, but one which transcends mere reason, or rather may be termed 'reason in her most exalted mood', a subtle combination of reason and emotion; for the higher forms of emotion, which are a kind of imaginative instinct, will often prove a guide to truth where pure reason fails. Seeking, then, for an interpretation of the universe that comprehends those elements in our nature which science, intent on her more limited purpose, is justified in neglecting, he dethrones reason from absolute monarchy among the faculties of man, and puts science in her justly subordinate place.

Wordsworth's attitude to science is entirely misconceived by those who regard him as its ignorant or contemptuous enemy. Among the inspirations of his life at Cambridge none was more lasting than the memory of the statue of Newton, with his prism and silent face—

> The marble index of a mind for ever
> Voyaging through strange seas of thought, alone,

and no one has paid more eloquent tribute than he to mathematics and 'its independent world, created out of pure intelligence'. He had indeed a poetic premonition of the part which mathematical physics would play in the advance of human knowledge, whilst to his mind, 'beset with images and haunted by itself', he knew the fascination and the relief afforded by mathematical abstraction:

> With awe and wonder did I meditate
> Upon the alliance of those simple, pure
> Proportions and relations with the frame
> And Laws of Nature, how they would become
> Herein a leader to the human mind . . .
> Yet from this source more frequently I drew
> A pleasure calm and deeper, a still sense
> Of permanent and universal sway
> And paramount endowment in the mind,
> An image not unworthy of the one
> Surpassing Life, which out of space and time,
> Nor touched by welterings of passion, is
> And hath the name of God. Transcendent peace
> And silence did await upon these thoughts.

The poet and the man of science were to him 'twin labourers, and heirs of the same hopes', and in his *Prelude* he has recorded a dream which, as De Quincey puts it, 'reaches the very *ne plus ultra* of sublimity, expressly framed to illustrate the eternity . . . of those two hemispheres, as it were, that compose the total world of human power, mathematics on the one hand, and poetry on the other'.

But since man is a spiritual being, poetry, with all it stands for, takes precedence of science. For just as in his youth Wordsworth had been conscious of influences of which science takes no account, so in the crisis of his life, when his hopes for humanity had failed him and his spiritual life ran dry, he found that the abstract truths of mathematics, to which he turned in despair as the one rock of certainty, availed him nothing; and only gradually did he regain his mental equilibrium when those elements in his nature which he had ruthlessly sought to expel, reasserted their sovereignty.

Yet this experience did not lead him to repudiate

science, but rather to define the just limits of her domain. With this intent he exposes the shallowness of the mind that is wholly satisfied with mechanical analysis; hence his oft-quoted aphorism 'we murder to dissect;' hence, too, those lines that have pained the susceptibilities of many a scientist, in which the physician is held up to scorn as a 'fingering slave,

> One who would peep and botanise
> Upon his mother's grave'.

But this is no more an attack on botanical science than the portrait which precedes it, of the 'man of purple cheer, right plump to see', is an attack on the Church of England. The offending lines, read in their context, are merely a satirical exposure of scientific curiosity where, as most of us would agree, it is out of place. Elsewhere Wordsworth expresses strong disagreement with those who held that the habit of analysing and anatomizing was necessarily destructive of other and higher faculties. On the contrary,

'Admiration and love,' he says, 'to which all knowledge truly vital must tend, are felt by men of real genius in proportion as their discoveries in natural philosophy are enlarged; and the beauty of form in plant or animal is not made less but more apparent as a whole by more accurate insight into its constituent properties and powers.'

This is indeed one of the greatest gifts of science:

> Happy is he who lives to understand
> Not human nature only, but explores
> All natures,—to the end that he may find
> The law that governs each; and where begins
> The union, the partition where, that makes
> Kind and degree, among all visible Beings . . .
> Up from the creeping plant to sovereign man.

Every isolated step in the advance of knowledge has its own intrinsic value: its supreme value depends on its correlation with the sum of human knowledge, so that it corrects and enriches our understanding of life as a whole. So conceived, the triumphs of science may become as fruitful a theme for the poet as any other field of human adventure; nay, without the poet's aid they will not be fully realized. The scientist, as such, excludes all sense of ultimate values—they are not his concern; whereas, says Wordsworth, it is the peculiar function of the poet 'to carry sensation into the midst of the objects of science itself', or to transfer pure thought into that world of imagination, of combined thought and feeling, in which the life of the spirit is lived. For 'poetry is the breath and finer spirit of all knowledge, the impassioned expression which is on the countenance of all science'.

And as Wordsworth recognized the place of scientific knowledge in the sum of man's intellectual experience, so he welcomed its application to the relief of man's estate:

> I exult to see
> An intellectual mastery exercised
> O'er the blind elements; . . . almost a soul
> Imparted to brute matter. I rejoice,
> Measuring the force of these gigantic powers
> That by the thinking mind have been compelled
> To serve the will of feeble-bodied Man.

But he protested against the identification of progress with their indiscriminate employment, which, ignoring paramount human values, sacrificed the claims of both beauty and humanity to 'gain, the master idol of the realm'.

In all this Wordsworth showed true prophetic insight. For just as many a social reform of to-day is a tardy attempt to correct or arrest the harm to our civilization which he foresaw, so science has herself outgrown that mechanistic view of the world against which he so passionately revolted. His belief in an 'active principle' subsisting in all natures, in whose creative power lies the true freedom of the universe, his mystical intuition of

> A motion and a spirit that impels
> All thinking things, all objects of all thoughts,
> And rolls through all things,

suggests a point of view not wholly incompatible with the latest speculations of the physicist. With confidence, therefore, Wordsworth welcomes the progress of knowledge. He has no desire to recall the illusions of the past, nor to shirk those

> Truths whose thick veil Science has drawn aside;

he knows that 'the universe is infinitely wide', and however far science may extend her frontiers, beyond them there will always remain a gulf, which 'imaginative faith alone can overleap'.

Of such a faith his age had need. The rapid advance of technology which marked the early nineteenth century, with its contributions to wealth and daily comfort, inevitably strengthened the hold of a facile materialism; the advance in scientific theory had already begun to shake, as never before, the foundations of religious belief. That spirit of unrest which two centuries earlier had haunted the mind of the poet Donne, was now to infect the whole educated world.

The sonnet of Wordsworth, from which I have just quoted, was written in 1833; it was his response to the epoch-making pronouncements of Lyell on the antiquity of the earth. Evolutionary conceptions of organic life were already in the air; they gained some popular vogue in 1844 from Robert Chambers's *Vestiges of Creation*, and in 1859 received their exhaustive and authoritative exposition in Darwin's *Origin of Species*, of which Huxley said with justice: 'It is doubtful whether any single book, except Newton's *Principia*, ever worked so great and so rapid a revolution in science,

or made so deep an impression on the general mind.'
The creation of the world, which theological tradition
had confidently dated 4004 B.C., was now put back into
a past infinitely remote, Adam and Eve and their
'delicious garden' were relegated to the pleasant, if
instructive, land of myth. And if the historicity of the
Bible were thus impugned in one capital instance, how
much else of its contents invited a similar interpretation? Obviously it could no longer be regarded as the
unimpeachable repository of literal fact; its true value
must largely depend, like that of other great literatures, on the measure of its power to stimulate and
satisfy the religious imagination. Moreover the in-
exorable laws of the struggle for existence and the survival of the fittest forced into prominence a nature 'red
in tooth and claw'—no new discovery indeed, but
hitherto little emphasized, and hard to reconcile with
the notion of a beneficent Creator

> Without whose tender care
> No sparrow falleth to the ground;

and lastly, man's inclusion in the evolutionary scheme
raised problems that admit no easy solution, as to man's
spiritual life, his origin and destiny, as to how far he can
be a free agent, or claim a personal relation with the
Deity.

Faced by these insistent questions only the most
obscurantist of ecclesiastics could emulate the ostrich:
the thinkers and poets were impelled to reconsider the
foundations of their belief. It was no easy task, and great
literature was born of the conflict. A later generation,
to whom the ideas of Lyell and Darwin are common-
places, has prated ignorantly of Victorian complacency;
but a little perception should help us to enter into the
minds of men who felt the ground on which they had
securely rested cut from under their feet, and to sympathize with their spiritual nostalgia at the loss of that

more definite creed which their reason forced them to renounce:

> The Sea of Faith,
> Was once too at the full, and round earth's shore
> Lay like the folds of a bright girdle furl'd;
> But now I only hear
> Its melancholy, long, withdrawing roar,
> Retreating to the breath
> Of the night wind, down the vast edges drear
> And naked shingles of the world.

Thus Matthew Arnold and his friend Clough, 'between two worlds, one dead, one powerless to be born', sought, in a creedless Christianity, a peace they could not find.

But the prevalent mood of the time found its well-nigh perfect expression in the poetry of Tennyson, and the spell that he exerted, not merely over the general public, but equally over the acutest thinkers and men of science, sprang from their recognition that in his search for a faith beyond the forms of faith he voiced their own doubts and aspirations.

'It lay', wrote the philosopher Henry Sidgwick, 'in the unparalleled combination of intensity of feeling with comprehensiveness of view and balance of judgement, shown in presenting the *deepest* needs and perplexities of humanity. We were absorbed in struggling for freedom of thought from the trammels of a historical religion; and what we sympathised with most, apart from the personal feeling, was the defence of honest doubt, the reconciliation of faith and knowledge, and generally the *forward* movement of the whole.'

Tennyson had always been deeply interested in natural science; Huxley, indeed, pronounced his insight into scientific method equal to that of the greatest experts. But the more obvious inferences drawn from scientific investigation:

> The stars, she whispers, blindly run,
>
> .   .   .   .   .
>
> So careful of the type she seems
> So careless of the single life,

ran counter to the instincts of his spiritual consciousness. The answer, he felt, could only lie in more knowledge; and pending that knowledge, man's sole refuge
was in faith—a faith which is no stolid adherence to
what science has disproved, but rather a faith in that
which is beyond both proof and disproof.

The modern sceptic pours scorn on Tennyson for
sheltering behind a faith he could not justify; but a
faith fully justified would not be faith at all, but knowledge. And yet, provided that faith is no mere lazy
acceptance of tradition, but the lively outcome of his
whole inner experience, a man has no more power, or
right, to abjure it than he has to reject the inferences
of his intellect. The two may seem inconsistent to an
outsider, he may himself be haunted with the fear that
they are inconsistent, and it was that fear that gave to
Tennyson's poetry its peculiar plangency of feeling.
Moreover, as he wavers in his faith, so too, at times, he
will doubt the validity of the verdict his reason urges
him to accept. Is our knowledge of the physical universe, confessedly incomplete as it is, to have the last
word on the spiritual life and destiny of man?

> Who loves not knowledge? Who shall rail
>   Against her beauty? May she mix
>   With men and prosper! Who shall fix
> Her pillars? Let her work prevail.
>
> But on her forehead sits a fire,
>   She sets her forward countenance
>   And leaps into the future chance,
> Submitting all things to desire.

Science, hardly less than theology, is tainted with
arrogant assumptions; her laws of nature are, after all,
no more than hypotheses which for the moment seem
best to fit the facts before her, and faced by other facts
she will propound other laws incompatible with her
former tenets. In her ceaseless quest for truth, she is

forced continually to modify, even to renounce, her
cherished theories:

> Our little systems have their day;
> They have their day and cease to be:
> They are but broken lights of thee,
> And thou, O Lord, art more than they.

Yet if science was thus disturbingly revolutionary in
the sphere of religion, in other regions of thought its
influence was both optimistic and conservative. Evolution, to Tennyson as to many others, implied progress,
but a progress which had its roots deep down in the
past; it thus encouraged an historical perspective in
the approach to all social and human problems; it emphasized, as never before, the influence of heredity and
of environment; whilst in the approach to literature it
enforced the value of tradition as opposed to ephemeral
caprice.

But the advance of knowledge makes not for unani-
mity but for diversity of human opinion, and how
differently different minds may react to the same
scientific data can be seen by contrasting their influence
upon some of the greatest among Tennyson's younger
contemporaries. George Meredith wholeheartedly welcomed the evolutionary doctrine, and drew from it a
buoyant optimism, untempered by any hankerings after
the supernatural. Earth was to him the great Mother
of all living things; the principle by which she educates
her children—natural selection through a conflict of
types, is but 'her cherishing of the best endowed'.
Through this conflict man has developed from mere
animalism, or 'blood', as Meredith terms it, to that
compound of blood, heart, and brain whose perfect
adjustment is the fulfilment of his life's purpose. But
he can only attain this harmony by keeping close to
reality; to ignore his kinship with Earth is folly: to
yearn beyond Earth for personal relation with the Lord
of Earth is delusion. By accepting her discipline, and

in mystical union with her, man gains all that he needs, the knowledge

> Of good and evil at strife,
> And the struggle upward of all,
> And [his] choice of the glory of life.

Thomas Hardy confronts the same universe with the obstinate questionings of tragic despair. The infinitude of space and time only emphasizes for him the helpless insignificance of man, the progress of the type only stresses the remorseless indifference to the individual. His hope for the future, and it is a dim hope, lies in 'evolutionary meliorism', which he defines as 'a minimum of loving-kindness, operating through scientific knowledge, and actuated by that modicum of free-will conjecturally possessed by organic life'.

A different outlook from either Meredith's or Hardy's characterizes Robert Bridges. Like Wordsworth, he realized how much that bears essentially on the riddle of life lay wholly outside the purview of science, and with a full appreciation of what science had accomplished in the years that divided them, he restated for his own age, and with a similar solution, the problem that Wordsworth had faced a century before.

Like Wordsworth, he admits no quarrel between science and poetry; he delights to record how science, 'comforting man's animal poverty, and leisuring his toil, hath humanized manners and social temper'; and no one has paid more lovely tribute than he to science's latest achievements. But science does not attempt to satisfy the spirit of man. When we ask how it is that our material bodies are capable of consciousness, of thought, and spiritual aspiration, she refuses to answer, not because she denies these mysteries, but because she can make nothing of them. But what if the clue lie in those very conditions of thought which pure reason rejects as delusive, i.e. in our instincts? Instinct in the

animals is purposeful, though the animal does not
understand the purpose; why should not man's higher
instincts be as true as those of the animals on their
lower plane? And prime among these instincts is the
instinct for beauty—

> The quality of appearances that thro' the senses
> wakneth spiritual emotion in the mind of man:
> And art, as it createth new forms of beauty
> awakneth new ideas that advance the spirit
> in the life of Reason to the wisdom of God.

Beauty is not illusory because it lies outside the scope
of science. To accept its suggestions as reality is indeed
an act of faith, but the scientist too works by faith
—faith in the validity of the mind's logical processes,
in the ultimate explicability of the physical world, in
the order of nature; the further faith of the poet, that
there is a purpose in that order, and that the order is
good, is but 'a reasonable trust in our deeper nature
and better desires, to doubt which were destructive of
reason herself':

> For beauty being the best of all we know
> sums up the unsearchable and secret aims
> of nature, and on joys whose earthly names
> were never told, can form and sense bestow;
> and man hath sped his instinct to outgo
> the steps of science, and against her shames
> imagination stakes out heavenly claims,
> building a tower above the head of woe.

The warmth of the welcome accorded to Bridge's
Testament of Beauty, far in excess of that which has
greeted any other serious imaginative work of our time,
bore clear testimony to the value, in a troubled world,
of his lofty and comprehensive spiritual experience;
more recent literature has given us nothing comparable
to it either in range or vision; and it is an arresting
paradox that at a time when contemporary science has
discarded its former materialistic outlook and when

theories of evolution, instead of throwing all their emphasis on man's affinity with lower types of life, trace a line of escape from the prison of matter to the full freedom of the spirit, imaginative literature should, as a whole, be deaf to its suggestions.

But the causes are not far to seek. In the first place the trend of scientific thought is largely obscured by its own materialistic triumphs. Science has become the victim of her own success. Dazzled by the wonder of the gifts which she deals out with so lavish a hand, man insults the dignity of her quest of truth by paying regard only to its practical by-products. In the second place the speculations of physical science have become so abstruse that they pass beyond the comprehension of the lay intelligence. The achievements of Copernicus, of Newton, of Darwin, were, at least in broad outline, explicable to the plain man; and while they destroyed his former illusions, gave him something in their place which, after his first disconcerting shock of surprise, proved more acceptable to his reason than the illusions they destroyed. But only a mind scientifically trained can grasp the quantum theory or relativity; and hence some time must elapse before the new ideas can be sufficiently assimilated by the layman to admit of adequate translation into the untechnical language of the literary artist, and thereby become a part of that intellectual and emotional experience which it is the function of literature to disseminate. It is true that eminent men of science, conscious of the difficulty, have attempted the task themselves, and some of their attempts have achieved the proud distinction of best sellers. But I am a little sceptical as to the number of readers who have fully understood either their arguments or their conclusions, nor is it derogatory to their scientific genius to suggest that they have not the supreme literary gift of 'carrying truth alive into the heart by passion'.

And further, the present distracted state of the world is not conducive to the absorption of new ideas. A generation that has grown up beneath the dark shadows of a disastrous war and a still more disastrous peace, breathes an atmosphere of disillusionment; it tends instinctively to call in question the meaning of life, to doubt, indeed, whether life can have a meaning. Justly critical of those whose folly and ignorance brought things to such a pass, they have seen the world as a Waste Land, peopled by hollow men; and realizing what man has made of man, they distrust the validity of the higher human impulses, and are attracted not to the more optimistic suggestions of physical speculation but to that branch of science which seems to justify their distrust. It was inevitable that biology should extend its researches from man's body to his mind, and explore the influence of physical upon mental states. But no department of science is fraught with more dangerous pitfalls for the amateur; and a dabbling in psycho-physics, by authors whose gifts are literary rather than scientific, has often warped their estimate of life and character. It is significant that their finest literary achievement has been in satire: alike in biography and in fiction the physical has been exaggerated at the expense of the spiritual; while criticism of the great literatures of the past has been tainted with a crude neurology, and its authors, ignorant of the sanity of true genius, have thrown more light upon their own personal frailty than upon the potential greatness of the human soul.

It is the calamity of our modern civilization, and may well prove its tragedy, that too large a portion of the world's available genius is absorbed by science, to the impoverishment not only of literature, but, even more, of that realm of practical affairs in which ideas are applied to life. More than a century ago, Shelley, himself a passionate devotee of science, diagnosed the malady of a world whose predicament was far less perilous than our own.

'We want', he said, 'the creative faculty to imagine what we know, we want the generous impulse to act what we imagine, we want the poetry of life. Our calculations have outrun conception—we have eaten more than we can digest. The cultivation of the sciences, which have enlarged the empire of man over the external world, has, for want of the poetic faculty, proportionally circumscribed those of the internal world, and man, having enslaved the elements, remains himself a slave.'

The gifts of science are double-edged, as we know to-day to our cost: it is not the fault of science that they are abused.

'It may be a forlorn hope,' wrote Thomas Hardy shortly before his death, 'that of an alliance, by means of the interfusing of poetry, between religion, which must be retained unless the world is to perish, and complete rationality, which must come unless also the world is to perish.'

But if contemporary literature has not yet risen to its great opportunity, it may be, as Hardy further suggests, because 'advance is never in a straight line, and may have moved back *pour mieux sauter*—drawn back for a spring'. And the signs are not without hope. In the meantime we have our heritage from the past. Great literature has this advantage over science, that it has a permanence co-extensive with human life and passion and aspiration. The science of yesterday is no longer science: it has already become history. Literature is always literature. Ptolemy's astronomy is out of date: the ecstasy with which he beheld the starlit heavens awakens its response in us to-day. Newton's *Principia* is in part superseded: but Shakespeare, despite modern psychology, does not 'abide our question'. Even where the ideas on which it is based are proved illusory, literature retains its power. The cosmography of the *Divine Comedy*, of *Paradise Lost*, of the Bible, has long been exploded, and in exploding it science has done them a service, for it has thrown into bolder relief their true poetic and spiritual content. In the past, their readers have often mistaken the husk for the kernel, and, battening on their dogma, failed to catch their inspiration: for us their power is manifest—'to raise the thoughts above sublunary cares and pleasures'.

In truth, man is a complex creature. Science was born from the insatiable curiosity of his intellect,

> To measure every wandering planet's course,
> Still climbing after knowledge infinite:

and science has flourished exceedingly. But man is also a poetical animal, and it has been wisely said that 'a savant who is not also a poet in soul and a religionist at heart is a feeble and unhappy creature'. On the balanced development of both parts of his nature depends his worth as an individual; in their just fusion as motive forces in society lies the measure of human progress.

VIII

THE ART OF CONVERSATION [1]

IN addressing a company gathered together in this building I need not elaborate the truism that to acquire some proficiency in our native tongue is a first essential of our education. Self-expression is a manifestation of life: it is also the chief means of self-development, and the only means by which we can communicate with the world about us. Yet some of us have so inadequately mastered this means of communication that we often fail to state with clearness and precision a simple fact; whilst few have that linguistic equipment which is necessary to a free and intelligent life in the larger world of ideas. For here the matter to be conveyed is less tangible; and the most exact and lucid language is demanded if the infinitely subtle shades and varieties of meaning are to be caught and apprehended.

This mastery of language is needed not only for the communication of ideas; it is needed equally for the preliminary processes of thought, and for the translation into a real consciousness of our own half-realized experience. It has well been said that for human beings as we know them, sight and hearing, knowledge and emotion, love and worship, are but rudiments of themselves until they are expressed. 'Nothing', says Bergson, 'is clear till we have put it into words, for words are the only means of translating impressions to the intellect. Hence the immense help expression gives to vision, in clarifying it. The growth of the power of language is not merely a technical development, it implies a growth of vision.' In the gift of speech and the proper use of it lies the vital distinction between man and the brute.

[1] A Lecture delivered in Abercromby House in the University of Liverpool, 11 November 1927.

Θεὸς δὲ ὁ λόγος. It is the divine element in man. Even the greatest masters of language have found, at times, their thought bounded and cut short by their inadequacy of speech. 'Words cannot exceed', says Sir Thomas Browne, 'where they cannot express enough. Even the most winged thoughts fall at the setting out, and reach not the portal of Divinity.'

But, after all, great writers can express more than we can; and so, for the deepest and most pregnant thought, the most vivid and imaginative representation of life, we turn to books, written for us by men the like of whom we do not often meet in our traffic with the world; and we look to their pages to supply us with what we lack in daily life. Then, if we have ideas of our own to communicate, or wish to record our own imaginative experience, we try, in our turn, to write it down for others.

But we often fail miserably. For though we may have understood and appreciated the language of these literary masters, their words have not really become our own. Unaccustomed to hear them on our own lips, or on the lips of others, they are no part of ourselves; they are really in a foreign language; and when we try to use them, we do it with a self-conscious effort that betrays itself in awkwardness and affectation.

The reason is that we have never learned to talk. There is, it is true, a general assumption prevalent that we can speak our own language; but how few of us can, or even make the effort! And as a result we exalt literature unduly at the expense of conversation, forgetting the essential relation between them. For after all the printed page is only a mechanical device for broadcasting, preferable indeed to the more modern system, which, as we degenerate, will largely take the place of reading, and preferable because it allows us to choose what we will hear, and does not force us to listen to any ugly fatuity that the general public mistakes for music or sense.

Good writing is only carefully considered speech. Long before man wrote, he talked; and that order must be repeated in every human being. The written language has its spring and its reservoir in the spoken language. It is only speech raised to a further perfection, purged of the inaccuracies caused by hurry, and compensating for the absence of those indefinable communications of personality, voice-inflection and gesture, by a greater lucidity, a purer outline, a more nicely expressive colour. We are apt to forget that much of the best literature takes the actual form of spoken language—in drama, in the great orators, in the conversations that bulk so large in novels, and that apart from this the diction of a great writer is close to that which would have actually passed his lips had he been discussing the same theme with an intelligent friend. The good writer is always, potentially at least, a good talker. He may indeed fail in talk from lack of readiness, or undue reserve, or distrust of present company. The tongue may falter where the pen runs swift and smooth. That was a just defence made by Addison when he remarked to one who blamed his silence, 'I may be short of small change, but I have a solid account at the bank'; and, indeed, it proved him a better talker than he knew. So Corneille's timidity of nature robbed his ordinary speech of that distinction which he gave to the conversation he wrote for others. 'No thought', says St. Evremond, 'is too daring for him to put into the mouth of a Greek or Roman, but when he speaks for a Spaniard or a Frenchman, his courage begins to ebb, and when he talks in his own person it wholly deserts him. He lends his old heroes all that is noble in his imagination, and you would say that he shrinks from making a personal use of what is his own, as though he were unworthy of it.' But Addison and Corneille are exceptions; for though the conversation of authors may not equal their writings, there is seldom a serious discrepancy; and when they are among their peers they talk far more like their books than is commonly supposed. To this, friends of both Meredith and Henry James, two of our most mannered writers, have borne ample witness.

Now one reason of our own failure, both in speech and writing, is that we allow our reading to have too little influence on our talk. The spoken vocabulary of a foreigner, who has learnt his English in part from books, often puts to shame our own. We do not practise in our ordinary conversation the use of that wide and exact vocabulary which our reading might help us to acquire. Sir Joshua Reynolds informs us that Dr. Johnson owed his mastery of language to his habit of striving on every occasion, and no matter how ignorant the company, to talk his best and to express himself in the most accurate and vivid phrases; but when we talk, for the most part, we only harden ourselves in a habit of slovenly and inexpressive speech. What true practice in talking entails is admirably summed up by the author of *Mark Rutherford*, himself among the purest writers of modern English, and certainly one of the best talkers that I was ever privileged to listen to. Mark Rutherford puts his view of the matter into his portrait of Mackay, one of his London friends:

'Mackay', he tells us, 'always insisted that there is no training more necessary for children than that of teaching them not merely to speak the truth in the ordinary, vulgar sense of the term, but to speak it in a much higher sense, by rigidly compelling, point by point, a correspondence of the words with the fact external or internal. He never would tolerate in his own children a mere hackneyed borrowed expression, but demanded exact portraiture; and nothing vexed him more than to hear one of them spoil and make worthless what he had seen, by reporting it in some stale phrase which had been used by everybody. This refusal to take the trouble to watch the presentment to the mind of anything which had been placed before it, and to reproduce it in its own lines and colours was, as he said, nothing but falsehood; and he maintained that the principal reason why people are so uninteresting is *not* that they have nothing to say. It is rather that they will not face the labour of saying in their own tongue what they have to say, but cover it up and conceal it in commonplace; so that we get, not what they themselves behold and what they think, but a hieroglyphic or symbol invented as a representative of a certain class of objects or emotions, and as inefficient to represent a particular object or emotion as x or y to set forth the relation of Hamlet to Ophelia. He would even exercise his children in this art of the higher truthfulness, and would purposely make them give him an account of something which he had seen and they had seen, checking them the moment he saw a lapse from originality.'

I shrewdly suspect that this admirable parent never existed outside the book in which he figures; anyhow, we, who were perhaps less fortunately fathered, must learn for ourselves the practice of conversation. But we can only learn it on the method that Mark Rutherford has laid down; that is, by never resting content in our speech with a vague and colourless approximation to our meaning, but striving to get as near it as we can. In doing this, we shall inevitably increase our vocabulary from the best books that we have read, and their language will become our own. Indeed, on what other source can we draw with any profit? Their vocabulary would not exist if there were no need for it, and we, with kindred ideas and emotions, have the same need for it as those from whom we learn it.

And we might begin by adding to our normal stock of adjectives, and by showing more discrimination in the use of them. When Coleridge was gazing on the Falls of the Clyde he observed to his neighbour that the scene before them was, in the strictest sense of the word, a sublime object, to which remark a lady assented with warmth, adding, 'Yes, it is not only sublime, it is beautiful, and absolutely pretty.' Coleridge's experience is not an uncommon one. Still more common is it to meet with persons who have only one ill-used, overworked epithet to express their approval, and one other for their censure, or only one such word for a certain space of time, after which, for reasons of fashion or caprice, that word is supplanted by another equally vague and equally inadequate. To such persons a play of Shakespeare's and a rag-time tune, the view from a mountain-top and an ice pudding, are alike 'topping', or 'enthralling', or 'great'. A young woman of my acquaintance, the wife of a distinguished literary man whose name, for obvious reasons, I do not divulge, remarks upon everything she likes, 'Isn't it too sweet?' Similarly at Oxford some years ago, where one would think they might know better, a large section of the community stigmatized everybody and everything that they dis-liked as 'squalid'. A robust young colleague of mine, who hails from a sister University, refers to the mildest changes and chances of this life as 'simply paralysing', and yet he still seems to have the use of his limbs. If Samuel Johnson had been their fellow-undergraduate they might have learned better. 'Sir,' said Mr. Evans to Johnson, 'I remember you would not let us say "prodigious".' And, turning to Boswell, he added, 'For even then, sir, he was delicate in language, and we all feared him.' It is sometimes argued that such a use of 'topping' or 'sweet', 'squalid', or 'paralysing', or 'pro-digious' is metaphorical, and so perhaps it was originally. But metaphor is only effective, or indeed metaphor at all, on the lips of those who are conscious of the word's literal meaning: when the metaphorical feeling is lost in its indiscriminate application the word has become a mere cliché; it is dead and, like the dead, should be allowed a decent burial. And the same holds true of slang, which on its first introduction to a language is often highly picturesque and imaginative. But it soon degenerates and becomes intolerable, though not, I think, so intolerable when it invents its own terms as

when it degrades old ones. For then useful and necessary words are emptied of their vital content, and the
language becomes irreparably the poorer and the less
expressive. Thus it is hardly possible to-day to give to
the word 'awful' its strict and forceful meaning, nor
does one person in a hundred, either in talk or writing,
observe any distinction between 'awful', 'terrible',
'horrible', 'tremendous'—all of them delicately differ-
entiated, and no one of them substituted for another
by authors with a nice sense of language. And as for
that really nice word 'nice'—Jane Austen, a century
ago, showed that its fate was already sealed.

'Do you not think *Udolpho* the *nicest* book in the world?' said
Catherine Morland.

'The nicest?' replied Henry Tilney, 'by which I suppose you
mean the neatest. That must depend on the binding.'

'I am sure,' said Catherine, confused, 'I did not mean anything wrong: but it *is* a nice book, and why should I not call
it so?'

'Very true,' said Henry, 'and this is a very nice day; and we
are taking a very nice walk; and you are two very nice young
ladies. Oh! it is a very nice word indeed! It does for everything.
Originally, perhaps, it was applied to express neatness, propriety,
delicacy or refinement: people were nice in their dress, in their
sentiments, or their choice. But now, every commendation on
every subject is compressed in that word.'

Having reduced our conversation to this deplorably
low level, we are in the habit of speaking somewhat
complacently of conversation as a lost art which throve
in an age of leisure, when people had not very much to
do. But it really belongs to an age of intellectual alert-
ness, and its decay among us is a sure sign of our intellectual torpidity. The fact is that with the rise in the
standard of physical comfort social intercourse has
tended to degenerate. Modern hospitality is often satisfied when it has performed the least necessary of its
duties. But a man can eat at home; he leaves his

arm-chair to get something that solitude cannot supply. And yet weak tea and snippets of sweet cake are a suggestive metaphor for what he finds in the intellectual fare of the average drawing-room, and the ampler and more substantial dinner table is as likely to starve his mind as to stuff his stomach. 'It is curious', wrote Mallock in *The New Republic*, 'that we are so careful of what goes into our mouths and so uncritical of what comes out of them.' Mallock suggested as a palliative to this evil a menu for conversation; but this is a poor remedy, for just as the cook would fail in his office if he provided nothing more solid than a menu, so the host who draws up a bill of intellectual fare will need to provide many of his guests not merely with topics for their talk but also ideas about them and words in which to express them. It is significant how often one hears a brilliant conversation in a novel or drama stigmatized as unrealistic. 'We don't talk like that,' we say. A remark best met by two rejoinders, 'Don't you wish we did?' and 'Are you sure that because we don't, no one else does?' Thus Wordsworth has often been attacked for saying that the language of poetry should be the language of *real men* in a state of emotional or intellectual excitement, rather than conventional, so-called poetic, language. It is not my business at this moment either to agree or disagree with him, but merely to suggest that before we criticize his statement we must have some idea of what he meant by a 'real' man, and how a 'real man' talks. Are we to imagine that on his rambles with Coleridge over the Quantock Hills, or in London on his visits to Lamb, both of them 'real men', he was content with the level of conversation to which we are accustomed in the drawing-room or the University corridors?

I need hardly remind you that this affected contempt for stimulating and lively talk, and the general inability for it, are of modern growth. The Greeks, of all nations the most intellectually alert, were great talkers: in the absence of books their education was conducted viva voce. Youths frequented the academies of the philosophers, who talked with them and encouraged them to argue and dispute. The matchless lucidity, beauty, and subtlety of the Greek language are partly due to the fact that it was essentially an instrument of talk, that it was written *by* men who were talkers *for* men who could themselves talk, and could therefore appreciate the finest shades of language. So, too, in the Latin schools of rhetoric the young Roman learnt to dispute, to assume the role of different well-known characters, real or imaginary, and to improvise speech or dialogue suited to their situation. Thus they trained their natural gift for speech, and their power over language was at least commensurate with their ideas. The general level of talk, even upon the most trivial matters, could not have been unaffected by this training. Whatever they had to say they could say well.

So it was in the earlier days of our own country. The Renaissance brought to England not only knowledge and a widening of interests, but a quickening of the intelligence, which bore rich social fruit. Castiglione's *Courtier* was among the most popular of books. It discoursed of all subjects on which an educated man might wish to discourse, and, what is more significant still, it treated them in conversational form, thus exerting its influence on the style of conversation as well as upon its subject-matter. The dialogue became a favourite form of literature, largely because it was closer to actuality than the more elaborate and pretentious treatise. The lively *Colloquies* of Erasmus are a case in point. Another is Ascham's *Toxophilus*, ostensibly a book on archery, but in the manner of conversation drifting leisurely along to deal with much besides. And Lyly's *Euphues*, which ousted lap-dogs from the warm knees of court ladies, was prized, not for its story, or even for its sentiments, but for its long protracted dialogues, which set a standard for polite conversation, so that to talk euphuistically became a fashionable craze. It was a foolish craze, no doubt, but affords proof enough that the Elizabethan took his conversation seriously, and regarded it as an art. These absurdities of fashion and affectations of style are only a perversion of a true instinct—the desire to develop to the utmost our natural gift for expression, to make intercourse lively and intellectual. And further, conversation was fully recognized as an essential means of self-improvement. Spenser's ideal courtier, the perfect and complete man, after practising his body in horsemanship and athletic exercise, and after gaining knowledge from private study,

> To enrich the storehouse of his powerful wit,

increases that knowledge, and brings it to excellence, 'through wise speeches and grave conference'. Bacon, who took all knowledge for his province, thought it worth while to set down short notes for civil conversation, part of which he afterwards remodelled into a pregnant essay *Of Discourse*, whilst he opens his essay on *Studies* by impressing upon us the interdependence of reading, writing, and talking, as all of them essential to a full training for life. 'Reading maketh a full man, conference a ready man, writing an exact man.'

Naturally, then, the man of letters set a special value upon talk as the living counterpart of his own calling. 'What things were done at the Mermaid', and what words were heard there!

> So nimble, and so full of subtle flame
> As if that every one from whence they came
> Had meant to put his whole wit in a jest,
> And had resolved to live a fool, the rest
> Of his dull life—

There was talk, indeed, when Ben Jonson sate lording

it among his tribe, till perchance Will Shakespeare made
his appearance, when even the rare Ben Jonson seemed
but a heavy Spanish galleon beside the nimbler English
man-of-war. Even the graver, less companionable
Milton loved good talk, and would go far to seek it.
An early biographer attributes Milton's residence abroad
to his desire for converse with men of culture and
learning, 'because he realised that the study of never so
many books without the advantages of conversation
serves only to render a man either a stupid fool or an
insufferable pedant'. The coffee-houses of the late
seventeenth and eighteenth centuries carried on the
good traditions of the Mermaid: Wills's, the famous
resort of Dryden; White's, the club of the politicians;
Buttons', where Addison 'gave his little senate laws',
were but a few of the public places where men could
gather to talk and listen. Addison calls attention to the
value to men of genius of social intercourse with their
equals, and attributes the fact that 'men of genius in
the same way of writing seldom rise up singly, but at
certain periods of time appear together, and in a body',
to the stimulus of their talk one with another. What
he found to be his own personal experience might also,
within natural limitations, be ours. It should certainly
be our aim as educated men to screw up a peg or two
the level of social intercourse.

For though good talkers still are found, they are
certainly less common than formerly, and less fully
recognized at their true worth. For nowadays, good
lively talk, if it has no practical aim in view, is often
contemptuously dismissed as 'talking for talking's sake'.
But if conversation is an art, for what better reason
could one talk than for talking's sake? Of course, what
is usually so spoken of is not really talk; it is mere
chatter. And it is because of the growth and pre-
dominance of chatter that we have tended to shift our
admiration from the Elizabethan ideal, the man who

could both act and talk, to that enigmatic creature whom we call the strong silent man, who is often thought strong only because he is silent. This glorification of the inarticulate has perils which my quotation from Bergson has already exposed. That man who cannot or will not explain himself is assuredly a dangerous idol, as well as an enemy to the amenities of life.

But a proper command of language is not the only requisite for conversation. For just as it takes two to make a friendship, so it takes at least two to make a conversation. The good talker has not only a gift of speech, but that social temper which makes his talk delightful to other men; and this, unlike the gift of language, is as much a matter of character as of intellect and imagination. It might be summed up as the gift of alert and intelligent sympathy, and the failure to attain it takes many different forms. Far worse enemies to conversation even than strong silent men are those who in one way or another talk as befits not time, and place, and company. It would be well, perhaps, that I should allude to one or two of these, in order that we may avoid them, or, if that is impossible, at least avoid becoming like them ourselves.

Thus obviously, the quarrelsome man, however voluble his rhetoric, is not a talker. He is an Appius

> who reddens at each word you speak
> And stares tremendous with a threatening eye,
> Like some fierce tyrant in old tapestry.

Our most innocent platitude he receives as a deadly insult to himself, and naturally, when he has bitten off our heads, we are left with no tongues to wag. Pepper and vinegar are doubtless sound ingredients in a challenge to mortal combat; our familiar intercourse we must be content to season with a sprinkling of Attic salt.

But others, more kindly in intention, are almost

equally fatal to true conversation. Such is the incorri-
gible funny man, with his ready-made and tedious
attempts at wit, who like a public entertainer distracts us
from the matter in hand by his eternal comic patter.
'Let the doors be shut upon him, that he may play the
fool nowhere but in's own house!' It is our own fault
if we follow him there.

And such is the man who in overweening pride at his
command of language harangues us in rounded periods,
as though we were a public meeting. This is an outrage
on the decencies of private life. It was Mr. Gladstone's
weakness, which Queen Victoria could never forgive
him, that he insisted in addressing her as though she
were the House of Commons. Mr. Gladstone's first
ancestor, our general parent Adam, fell into a like error,
though, indeed, *he* had this excuse, that there was then
no House of Commons on which to practise his unseasonable eloquence. Yet we must admit that Eve did
not resent it. Indeed, she once went so far as to pay
him the finest compliment that ever rejoiced the ears
of talker: 'With thee conversing I forget all time.' But
then Eve, unlike Queen Victoria, had no Mr. Disraeli
to pay her compliments; nay, further, she had never
experienced what real talk might be. For whatever else
may have degenerated since the age of innocence, the
art of conversation has certainly improved, and to those
who wish to ingratiate themselves with the daughters
of Eve I hesitate to recommend Adam as a model.

And next I would censure the man who talks too
much. 'I wonder you will still be talking, Signor Benedick, nobody marks you,' says Beatrice in *Much Ado
About Nothing*, quite unjustly, for she hangs on every
word he utters, and knows well enough that there is no
better talker than Benedick in all Messina. It is odd
that the wittiest reproofs of unseasonable babbling have
been directed against the most brilliant talkers in literature. Thus, in *The Way of the World* Witwood remarks

of Millamant, 'I know a lady that loves talking so incessantly that she won't give an echo fair play. She has
that everlasting rotation of tongue that an echo must
wait till she dies before it can catch her last words.' We
have been fortunate indeed if none of our acquaintance
merit these censures more truly than Benedick or Millamant. For the bore, who pours forth a stream of
irrelevancy, hopping from one subject to another irrespective of its interest to anyone but himself, asking
questions to which even he does not want an answer,
simply from an inordinate love for his own voice—this
man is no new portent, he has been with us since the
beginning of time. Ancient Greece knew him well, and
pilloried him as he deserved. 'On his way to Athens',
says Theophrastus, 'he will ask the first man he meets
how hides and salt fish are selling, and whether the
magistrate celebrates the new moon to-day, adding
immediately that he means to get his hair cut when he
gets to town, and to buy some salt fish from Archias as
he goes by'; and this type of bore hardly differs from
that merely loquacious man who constantly ejaculates
'How much one gets from a little talk, to be sure!' and
whose children say to him at bedtime, 'Papa, chatter to
us, that we may fall asleep!' 'Such a man', says Butler, 'is
a siren unto himself, and has no way to escape shipwreck
but by having his *mouth* stopped instead of his ears.'

Closely allied to the loquacious bore, and equally
incapable of conversation, is he whose remarks bear no
relation with the ideas of his interlocutor, but who
simply pursues his own thread unaffected by the in-
attention of the other. Such were Mrs. Thorpe and
Mrs. Allen, as Jane Austen has presented them, who
'spent their whole time in what they *called* conversation,
but in which there was no interchange of opinion and
not often any resemblance of subject, for Mrs. Thorpe
spoke continually of her children, and Mrs. Allen of her
gowns'.

And yet sympathy, though essential, must never become self-effacement. Conversation is the play of mind upon mind, and not the impress of a die upon a mass of shapeless wax. It was the tragedy in the life of Mr. Shandy that Mrs. Shandy would never refuse her assent to any proposition he laid before her, merely because she did not understand it. 'This', says Tristran Shandy, 'was an eternal source of misery to my father, and broke the neck, at the first setting out, of more good dialogues between them than the most petulant contradiction would have done.' That was no true conversation which ensued one night between them as to the advisability of putting their little son into knickerbockers:

'We should begin', said my father, turning himself half round in bed, and shifting his pillow a little towards my mother's, as he opened the debate, 'We should begin to think of putting this boy into breeches.'

'We should so,' said my mother.

'We defer it, my dear,' quoth my father, 'shamefully.'

'I should think we do, Mr. Shandy,' said my mother.

'Not but what the child looks extremely well,' said my father, 'in his vests and tunics.'

'He does look very well in them,' replied my mother.

'And for that reason it would be almost a sin,' added my father, 'to take him out of 'em.'

'It would so,' said my mother.

'But indeed, he is growing a very tall lad,' rejoined my father.

'He is very tall for his age, indeed,' said my mother.

'I *can not* (making two syllables of it) imagine,' quoth my father, 'who the deuce he takes after.'

'I cannot conceive, for my life,' said my mother.

'Humph!' said my father.

(The dialogue ceased for a moment.)

'I am very short myself,' continued my father gravely.

'You *are* very short, Mr. Shandy,' said my mother.

'Humph!' quoth my father to himself, a second time: in muttering which he plucked his pillow a little farther from my mother's—and turning about again, there was an end of the debate for three minutes and a half.

'When he gets these breeches made,' cried my father in a higher tone, 'he'll look like a beast in them.'

'He *will* be very awkward in them at first,' replied my mother.

'And 'twill be lucky, if that's the worst on't,' added my father.

'It *will* be *very* lucky,' answered my mother.

'I suppose,' replied my father, making some pause first, 'he'll be exactly like other people's children.'

'Exactly,' said my mother.

'Though I shall be sorry for that,' added my father; and so the debate stopped again.

'They should be of leather,' said my father, turning him about again.

'They will last him,' said my mother, 'the longest.'

'But he can have no linings to 'em,' replied my father.

'He cannot,' said my mother.

' 'Twere better to have them of fustian,' quoth my father.

'Nothing can be better,' quoth my mother.

'Except dimity,' replied my father.

' 'Tis best of all,' replied my mother.

'One must not give him his death, however,' interrupted my father.

'By no means,' said my mother. And so the dialogue stood still again.

'I am resolved, however,' quoth my father, breaking silence the fourth time, 'he shall have no pockets in them.'

'There is no occasion for any,' said my mother.

'I mean in his coat and waistcoat,' cried my father.

'I mean so, too,' replied my mother.

'Though if he gets a gig or top—Poor souls! it is a crown and sceptre to them—they should have where to secure it.'

'Order it as you please, Mr. Shandy,' replied my mother.

'But don't you think it *right*?' added my father, pressing the point home to her.

'Perfectly,' said my mother, 'if it pleases you, Mr. Shandy.'

'There's for you,' cried my father, losing temper. 'Pleases me! You will never distinguish, Mrs. Shandy, nor shall I ever teach you to do it, betwixt a point of pleasure and a point of convenience.'

How far the prevalence of Mrs. Shandys makes for the peace of English domestic hearths I am not psychologist enough to determine, but it is clear enough that they destroy all chance of stimulating conversation. Most of us indeed would not have had the persistent optimism of Mr. Shandy, but would have given up the attempt after the first round instead of pursuing it into the fourth.

But if a too acquiescent mood is fatal to conversation, the inability to understand the mood of our friend and enter into his attitude of mind is almost as bad. Our temper must be suited to the occasion. A too literal mind may have its valued place in philosophical dialogue, serving to keep us to the point to which we steer with perhaps too devious a course: it will only be a curse when conversation is on matters that touch the feelings. We must not too closely scrutinize the language of the heart. Thus Godwin was clearly in error when, receiving the happy news of the birth of his daughter, he hurried in to ask his wife Mary Wollstonecraft how she did, and to her happy ejaculation, 'Oh, I am now in heaven!' replied, 'By which expression I understand you to mean that you experience a sensible relief from suffering.' The affairs that come home to our bosoms cannot be carried on in language so carefully guarded; and after this, we are not surprised to learn that Godwin and his wife, genuinely devoted to one another as they were, found it more convenient to live in separate houses, meeting regularly for serious and well-ordered discussion, of which, without doubt, Godwin was an accomplished master.

But as a rule the man of literal mind has not the excuse of Godwin's peculiar type of intellect. His failing is rather a total lack of interest in anything unless he can believe that it corresponds with what is solid and actual. He will spoil your finest flight of fancy by asking whether you really mean it; he has no ear for your

most brilliant narration unless he can be assured that
it is what he calls true—as if he knew what truth was
any better than jesting Pilate. Such a man has no
social uses. He should keep to his likes for company.
Nor can he stray with safety into the realm of books.
Bradshaw, which should be symbolically bound in
sheepskin or calf, is the only kind of literature that he
is capable of understanding, and even here he should
be warned not to read the advertisements. Such characters afford us exquisite comedy upon the stage or in the
pages of a novel, and even when they cross our horizon
in daily life, provided that their passage is swift and we
have a friend at hand to whom we may confide our
impression of them. And yet how often we suffer from
them. Among Bunyan's pilgrims 'there was a young
woman, and her name was Dull'. Unfortunately,
though Bunyan does not record it, she married and had
prolific offspring.

From the melancholy examples I have given you of
failures to attain to the art of conversation, we can
learn at least how not to talk. And we can cull, too,
some positive hints. Thus it is evident that one of the
first lessons for the talker to learn is the art of listening.
For the egoist—and all of us are in a measure egoists—
this is a hard lesson. How many persons, when you are
speaking to them, are wholly occupied in thinking out
their own next remark, and when they have hit upon it,
as though fearing so good a thing should be lost, break
in with an irrelevancy that destroys the ordered development of good converse? But the good talker is always
a good listener; like the Arténice of La Bruyère, he is
sensitive to the least of your suggestions, and embellishes
it with his fancy, turning what was, perhaps, a commonplace as you uttered it into a lively truth, so that instead
of feeling despondent at the poverty of your own
remarks you are elated at finding how much more pregnant is your discourse than you had thought it. In the

alembic of his wit or wisdom he distils your molten dross into gold, and with such subtle skill that you feel the gold to be not his, but yours, or at least that you are an equal partner in the alchemy. By such delicate flattery, at the same time as he gives the finest example of his own skill, he stimulates the best that is in you, goading you on to further effort alike by alert and intelligent agreement, and by provocative or wayward opposition. Falstaff was the prince of wits, not merely because he was witty himself, but because he was the cause of wit in other men. Conversation is a tournament rather than a combat, and when all is over its quality is tested by the number of those who have acquitted themselves with honour, and not by counting the corpses of the slain.

But as an ounce of example is worth many pounds of precept, I will now read to you a perfect conversation. It was held between two persons who, though not what we should call educated, had yet the supreme gift for talk. It is a love scene between Peggeen and Christy Mahon in Synge's *Playboy of the Western World*, and Synge has assured us that their language is such as is in daily use among the country people of Ireland. Love-making, I suppose, is usually rather below than above the average of talk, for the speakers are apt to fall back on what are called 'the silent depths that lie below speech'. That dialogue, overheard, to his infinite disgust, by Mr. Punch's cynical old gentleman, is hardly an exaggerated travesty of real life: 'Darling!' 'Yes, darling?' 'Oh, nothing, darling, only *darling*, darling!' This is probably a truer transcript of the ways of the world than the more elaborate colloquies that adorn the pages of our best fiction. But artists are right in insisting on the immense opportunities offered by such an occasion to those who have the gift of tongues. In Synge's dialogue you will notice just those qualities that make the essence of all good talk—the play of fancy in each speaker, and the manner in which each catches up the words of the other, developing his points, and egging him on to still higher flights of eloquence:

CHRISTY. When the airs is warming, in four months or five, it's then yourself and me should be pacing Neifin in the dews of night the times sweet smells do be rising, and you'd see a little, shiny new moon, maybe, sinking on the hills.

PEGGEEN. And it's that kind of poacher's love you'd make, Christy Mahon, on the sides of Neifin, when the night is down?

CHRIS. It's little you'll think if my love's a poacher's, or an earl's itself, when you'll feel my two hands stretched around you, and I squeezing kisses on your puckered lips, till I'd feel a kind of pity for the Lord God is all ages sitting lonesome in His golden chair.

PEG. That'll be right fun, Christy Mahon, and any girl would walk her heart out before she'd meet a young man was your like for eloquence, or talk at all.

CHRIS. Let you wait, to hear me talking, till we're astray in Erris, when Good Friday's by, drinking a sup from a well, and making mighty kisses with our wetted mouths, or gaming in a gap of sunshine, with yourself stretched back into your necklace, in the flowers of the earth.

PEG. I'd be nice so, is it?

CHRIS. If the mitred bishops seen you that time, they'd be the like of the holy prophets, I'm thinking, do be straining the bars of Paradise to lay eyes on the Lady Helen of Troy, and she abroad, pacing back and forward, with a nosegay in her golden shawl.

PEG. And what is it I have, Christy Mahon, to make me fitting entertainment for the like of you, that has such poet's talking, and such bravery of heart?

CHRIS. Isn't the light of seven heavens in your heart alone, the way you'll be an angel's lamp to me from this out, and I abroad in the darkness, spearing salmons in the Owen or the Carrowmore?

PEG. If I was your wife I'd be along with you those nights, Christy Mahon, the way you'd see I was a great hand at coaxing bailiffs, or coining funny nicknames for the stars of night.

CHRIS. You, is it? Taking your death in the hailstones, or in the fogs of dawn.

PEG. Yourself and me would shelter easy in a narrow bush
. . . but we're only talking, maybe, for this would be a poor,
thatched place to hold a fine lad, is the like of you.

CHRIS. If I wasn't a good Christian, it's on my naked knees
I'd be saying my prayers and paters to every jackstraw you have
roofing your head, and every stony pebble is paving the laneway
to your door.

PEG. If that's the truth I'll be burning candles from this out
to the miracles of God that have brought you from the South
to-day, and I with my gowns bought ready, the way I can wed
you, and not wait at all.

CHRIS. It's miracles, and that's the truth. Me toiling a long
while, and walking a long while, not knowing at all I was drawing
all times nearer to this holy day.

PEG. And myself, a girl, was tempted often to go sailing the
seas till I'd marry a Jew-man, with ten kegs of gold, and I not
knowing at all there was the like of you drawing nearer, like the
stars of God.

CHRIS. And to think I'm long years hearing women talking
that talk, and this the first time I've heard the like of your voice
talking sweetly for my own delight.

PEG. And to think it's me is talking sweetly, Christy Mahon,
and I the fright of seven townlands for my biting tongue. Well,
the heart's a wonder; and, I'm thinking, there won't be our like
in Mayo, for gallant lovers, from this hour to-day.

What wonderful talk we have here! Christy Mahon
and Peggeen were fated to part, and there is something
to us of tragedy in Peggeen's last heart-broken words
'I've lost my playboy of the western world!' Hence we
can only conjecture how long they would have been
able to keep it up. It may be, if they had married, that
their lives would have been less peaceable than those of
the Shandys or the Godwins, who lived 'in tolerable
concord, with occasional bickerings, as befits near relations'. But we can safely predict that at the least they
would have had few dull moments to endure. And it
would always have been a joy to meet them.

It would be a joy to meet us if only we took some
pains to cultivate our gift of speech. Both for our own

sakes and for the sake of those with whom we come in contact it is well worth while. Recall what Pope owed to his conversation with Bolingbroke:

> Formed by thy converse happily to steer
> From grave to gay, from lively to severe,
> Correct with spirit, eloquent with ease,
> Intent to reason, and polite to please.

Here is the whole art of conversation. Its subject matters little: 'The good talker', says La Fontaine, 'is like the bee who gathers honey alike from every different flower'; perhaps his greatest art is shown when the subject seems least promising. Swift could write finely upon a broomstick, and would have talked equally well upon it.

> The daily round, the common task
> Will furnish all we need to ask.

To be able to talk well about trifles, and play upon them with a deft fancy, to turn the flash-light of humour upon our petty worries and disappointments, is to lift for a moment the dull and weary weight

> Of all this unintelligible world;

for the world only weighs heavy upon us because of its materiality. The *esprit* of good talk spiritualizes the material; and so spiritualized, what matter if it be unintelligible?

But naturally, as serious human beings, we shall not always be satisfied with skimming upon the surface, and our conversation will sometimes treat of those matters which concern us more deeply, of the problems that continually face us in society—of man, of nature, and of human life. Let us not be content to muse on these in solitude, and then write essays or sermons about them. 'It has always appeared to me', says Landor, 'that conversation brings forth ideas readily and plenteously, and that the ideas of one person no sooner come out than another's follow, whether upon the same

side or the opposite.' Thus we shall be the richer ourselves if we give our best thoughts to others. 'Occasion,'
says Montaigne, 'company, yea, the very rising and
falling of my own voice, draws more from my mind
than I can find therein when by myself I endeavour to
employ the same. My words are better than my writings, and this also hapneth unto me, that where I seek
myself, I find not myself, and I find myself more by
chance, than by the search of mine own judgment.'
Conversation is a contest in which every competitor
may win a prize. But to gain the prize we must go
whole-heartedly into it. There must be no holding back.
Many of us fail through undue sensitiveness. We fear
that we shall be worsted in argument, and at the first
show of opposition we imitate the uncompanionable
snail who,

> his tender horns being hit,
> Retreats into his shelly cave with pain.

We cherish our own ideas too fondly to risk their
exposure and defeat. They may be poor things, but
they are our own. Or perchance we have felt the force
of Sir Thomas Browne's warning that we may be 'in
possession of truth as of a citadel and yet be forced to
surrender' and that, therefore, ' 'tis far better to enjoy
her with peace than to hazard her on a battle'. But this
is a churlish modesty, and, like much modesty, is but the
reverse side of the medal of conceit. For if it is modest
to doubt our own prowess in argument it is surely the
height of arrogance to be confident in our possession of
truth. Wiser than Browne was Montaigne. 'We are
born', he says, 'to quest and seek after truth: to possess
her belongs to a greater power.' Truth will not dawn
if I establish my point, or you yours; still less if each of
us withhold the truth that he thinks is in him: in the
clash of the two, as with one flint upon another, some
faint spark may flicker across our twilight. And if the

worst come to the worst, and we are forced to give
ground, we can at least comfort ourselves with the
time-honoured reflection that

> He that complies against his will
> Is of his own opinion still.

But indeed, we should not be over anxious to convince. Without some desire to convince good talk is,
perhaps, impossible, but though we play for victory, we
should play also for the game. The game is greater than
the prize. Excellent and stimulating talk comes often
from those who are ever ready to defend a position in
which they know that they will be worsted. Theirs is
the very knight-errantry of talk; they devote their lives
to the succour of weak and distressed ideas. And such
talk has its higher uses. For the defence of a position in
which you do not yourself believe may serve to bring
out the truth from the lips of others, and so to convince
you more firmly of what before you only half-credited.
After all, you are not on oath, and no man can be called
a liar who does not pretend to tell the truth.

But the best conversation comes from those who
really and whole-heartedly express themselves. I do not
say talk about themselves, which is a very different and
often a very tedious thing. Sincerity in talk is worth a
good deal of mere cleverness, or brilliance in attack and
defence. Some people are afraid to say what they really
mean, lest, as they put it, they should give themselves
away. But of all social meannesses this is the worst.
Why should we give away nothing in our talk, or if we
give anything, only give away other people? What
have we to give, in the last resort, except ourselves?
Conversation is like that life of which it is the expression,
in that it is an adventure in which we must be prepared
to take our risks. It is no good playing for safety. One
splendid indiscretion is worth a world of caution. It is
only by that intercommunion of minds that comes from

sincere and unreserved talk that true friends are made
out of chance acquaintances, and are kept as friends;
and life has nothing better to offer than its friendships.
And here I may add a warning. Many who will make
an effort to talk their best in a casual company of
strangers delude themselves into thinking that among
friends they need make no effort. But if our friends are
worth having, nothing that we give them can be good
enough for them, and the best thing that we can give,
either in our life or in our talk, is only ourselves. The
talk of friends who have, as friends must have, community of interest, and have, as all individuals must
have, divergence of point of view is the purest of
human pleasures. 'It is', says Montaigne, 'more delight-
some than any other motion in our life. And that is the
reason why if I were forced to choose, I would rather
yield to lose my sight than forgo my hearing and my
speech.' Conversation is of all the arts the one which
contributes most fully to the sum of human happiness.

St. Augustine in his *Confessions* has drawn a happy
picture of a society of friends who had cultivated the
art of conversation.

'What chiefly', he says, 'took my mind in their company was
the talk, the laughter, the courteous mutual deference, the
reading of pretty books together, the comradeship sometimes in
jest, and otherwise seriously in earnest, the differences that left
no sting, as of a man differing from himself, the spice of disagreement which seasoned the monotony of consent. Each by turns
would instruct or listen, the absent were always missed, the
present always welcome. Such tokens springing up from the
hearts of friends, and displayed by a word, a gesture, an expression, by a thousand pretty complaisances, supply the heat which,
as it sets souls ablaze, welds them together and makes one of
many.'

No society offers better opportunities for stimulating
and productive talk than a College or University. I do
not, indeed, advocate talking in lectures, for there you

may be interrupted, nor in examinations, for that may be misconstrued; but at almost every other time and place academic conditions are well-nigh perfect. The words in which Tennyson recalls his happy days at Cambridge would be echoed by any intelligent graduate, looking back upon the best part of his life:

> Where once we held debate, a band
> Of youthful friends, on mind and art,
> And labour, and the changing mart,
> And all the framework of the land.
> When one would aim an arrow fair
> But sent it slackly from the string,
> And one would pierce an outer ring,
> And one an inner, here and there;
> And last, the master bowman, he
> Would cleave the mark. . . .

But I have spoken long enough; it is high time for the master to take bow in hand and speed his arrow from the string.

PRINTED IN
GREAT BRITAIN
AT THE
UNIVERSITY PRESS
OXFORD
BY
CHARLES BATEY
PRINTER
TO THE
UNIVERSITY